PREVENTING CREDIT CARD FRAUD

PREVENTING CREDIT CARD FRAUD

A Complete Guide for Everyone from Merchants to Consumers

Jen Grondahl Lee and Gini Graham Scott

ROWMAN & LITTLEFIELD
Lanham • Boulder • New York • London

Published by Rowman & Littlefield
A wholly owned subsidary of The Rowman & Littlefield Publishing Group,
Inc.
4501 Forbes Boulevard, Suite 200, Lanham, Maryland 20706
www.rowman.com

Unit A, Whitacre Mews, 26-34 Stannary Street, London SE11 4AB

British Library Cataloguing in Publication Information Available

Library of Congress Cataloging-in-Publication Data

Names: Lee, Jen Grondahl, author. | Scott, Gini Graham, author.
Title: Preventing credit card fraud : a complete guide for everyone from merchants to consumers /
    Jen Grondahl Lee and Gini Graham Scott.
Description: Lanham : Rowman & Littlefield, [2016] | Includes bibliographical references and
    index.
Identifiers: LCCN 2016039952 (print) | LCCN 2016053755 (ebook) | ISBN 9781442267992
    (cloth : alk. paper) | ISBN 9781442268005 (Electronic)
Subjects: LCSH: Credit —Security measures. | Credit card fraud—Prevention.
Classification: : LCC HG3755.7 .L44 2016 (print) | LCC HG3755.7 (ebook) | DDC 364.4—dc23
    LC record available at https://lccn.loc.gov/2016039952

Printed in the United States of America

CONTENTS

ABOUT THE AUTHORS

Jen Grondahl Lee is a successful bankruptcy attorney who has her own practice, Jen Lee Law, in San Ramon, California. She also assists clients with debt and credit card issues. Her practice is dedicated to helping small businesses and individuals figure out how to deal with debt issues and develop long-term plans for financial stability.

Jen helps her clients get back on track by exploring their financial problems and coming up with multiple solutions to get out of debt and restore their credit. Her knowledge about finances, business operations, and budgeting has helped many clients get the fresh start they needed to resolve their financial problems and become successful again. Jen is a member of the National Association of Bankruptcy Attorneys, the American Bankruptcy Institute, and local county bar associations. She speaks to various professional organizations on a regular basis.

Prior to law school, Jen worked in the insurance and financial planning industry and held various security licenses from the National Association of Securities Dealers, now known as FINRA (Financial Industry Regulatory Authority) and insurance licenses (California Life & Health), along with several industry designations (Chartered Life Underwriter; Fellow, Life Management Institute; Associate, Customer Service; Associate, Insurance Regulatory Compliance; Associate, Reinsurance Administration).

In addition to her JD degree from University of Richmond, T.C. Williams School of Law, Jen has an MBA in global management and a BS in business management.

Gini Graham Scott had her own experience of being defrauded by two clients and published an article on the subject in the *Huffington Post*, "Protect Yourself against Credit Card Fraud by Clients and Customers," which is featured in the foreword.

Scott is a nationally known writer, consultant, speaker, and seminar leader, specializing in business and work relationships, professional and personal development, social trends, popular culture, lifestyles, and criminal justice. She has published over fifty books with major publishers, has published forty books under her own publishing label, Changemakers Publishing, primarily on popular business and self-help topics, and has licensed several dozen books for foreign sales, including the UK, Russia, Korea, Spain, and Japan. As a *HuffPost* regular columnist, she comments on social trends, new technology, and everyday life at www.huffingtonpost.com/gini-graham-scott. She has previously written several books on criminal justice and fraud topics, including *Scammed*, *The Truth about Lying*, and *Lies and Liars*.

As a ghostwriter, she has written dozens of proposals, books, articles, blogs, and PR materials for clients. She has also been a cowriter on several books, including *American Justice* with Paul Brakke and *At Death's Door* with Sebastian Sepulveda. As a marketing and promotion consultant, she has set up events attracting several hundred participants, many of these programs as an organizer and assistant organizer of six Meetup groups in the business, start-up, film, and social media communities in Los Angeles and San Francisco, with over ten thousand members. Most recently, she has written and developed a series on *Make More Money with Your Book* (http://www.makemoremoneywithyourbook.com), including four published books on creating workshops and seminars; conducting an online sales campaign; creating videos, podcasts, and audio books; and developing an ad, PR, and social media campaign.

In addition, she is a member of numerous business groups, including the Lafayette, Danville, and Concord Chambers of Commerce, and has recently participated in several fairs drawing thousands of participants, including Lafayette's biggest annual event, the Art and Wine Festival. Over the years, she has built up a personal database of over six thousand contacts in the business and film communities in L.A. and the Bay Area and does regular e-mails to these groups.

She is also a marketing associate with the Jones & O'Malley Public Relations Company, and as such does regular blasts to targeted media for her own books and for clients using the Cision database.

She has received national media exposure for her books, including appearances on *Good Morning America*, *Oprah*, *Montel Williams*, and CNN. She has been the producer and host of a talk show series, *Changemakers*, featuring interviews on various types of change.

As a filmmaker, she has written and produced over fifty short videos, and is the writer and executive producer of three films in release or in postproduction, including *Suicide Party #Save Dave*, *Driver*, and *At Death's Door*, based on the book of the same name.

FOREWORD

A lot has been written about fraud perpetrated by fraudsters around the world. Some get your credit card information and put bogus charges on it. Others lure you into signing up for what appears to be a good deal or free trial of a product, subscription, or service that then turns out not to be free. Consumers keep falling for these traps because so many of the fraudsters are so compelling.

Another credit card scam that has not received much attention is where clients and customers obtain products and services by using a credit card and later claiming fraud to get their money back. This is particularly a problem for merchants, service providers, professionals, and freelancers who get their clients online.

Since the early days of Internet commerce, I have run two mostly online businesses, where I do not meet most clients. Typically, they pay by a credit card, debit card, or PayPal; occasionally they mail a check. Since 2000, the model has worked well for my Internet-based business, where I write and ghostwrite for clients all over the world and also help clients find publishers, agents, and film industry contacts by sending e-mails for them to contacts who might be interested in their projects.

Over the past fifteen years, I have received only two complaints—one from a woman with a course, who later claimed she wanted something different from what I had written and another from a client who was unable to sell his book from a mailing I sent to publishers, for which, of course, there were no guarantees. In both cases, I proved I did the writing and mailings by providing voluminous e-mail exchanges, so I won my cases and kept my money.

But in the last year or so, the rules seem to have changed, perhaps due to the proliferation of Internet fraud cases (many of which are described at length on the FBI website.[1] Now it appears that a person who merely claims fraud usually will win, even in the face of extensive e-mail evidence to the contrary. However, there are some steps business people can take to reduce the potential for claims of fraud against them.

I began thinking about this problem after I got two complaints in the last four months from devious clients. In one case, a woman and her husband hired my e-mail service to pitch a book proposal, and after four dozen publishers and agents expressed interest, the husband asked me to review a proposal he had written. When I told him the proposal was badly written, he asked me to rewrite it. I rewrote much of it and charged the card number he had given me. He then asked me to write more, but his card was declined for the additional charge. The couple then claimed they had gone over budget and asked if I would take the balance in trade. After I said no, not only did they not pay the declined charge, they also filed a claim saying they had not authorized the original charge or participated in the transaction. So I sent my merchant account bank a detailed letter about our extensive exchanges along with 380 supporting pages of e-mails and material I had written to prove the charge was valid. My bank reversed the chargeback. But the couple then lied to their bank again, reaffirming their original claim. In the end, my bank reversed the reversal, so they got their money back. Compounding the fraud, I later learned that they used the proposal I had written to sell their book to a publisher.

Later, a loony client for whom I had written a bio and foreword for her book abandoned the project after a personal emergency. She, too, got her money back by claiming fraud, even though she had sent me an e-mail with her credit card information, authorizing me to charge it for doing the work she asked me to do.

Of course, there is plenty of fraud in the other direction as well. Consumers are doing more and more purchasing online and constantly giving their credit card information. Unfortunately, it is not always easy to tell the valid requests for payments from those that are not.

So what can consumers, merchants, service providers, professionals, and freelancers do to avoid being victimized by client and customer fraudsters in long-distance, online transactions?

1. As a consumer, when dealing with an unfamiliar company, check their website for detailed information about the company, its management, and its products or services, or try to talk to someone on the phone to verify if this company is real.
2. Get payments in cash, cashier's check, money order, or check.
3. Create a verified by Visa or MasterCard order form on your website, which the person has to sign online to authorize payment.
4. Ask a customer or client to sign an online purchase agreement form or send the signed form to you by fax or mail.
5. If you process credit card payments through a terminal or call it in to a processing service, ask for the security code, as well as the address and zip code, even if not needed to authorize payment. This added information can help show that the buyer authorized the payment and participated in the transaction.
6. Keep a copy of all e-mail exchanges and anything sent to you by mail, since this evidence can bolster your case.
7. File a report of the fraud—or attempted fraud if you win—with the appropriate agencies and reporting services. These might include the Better Business Bureau for the region where the client's or customer's business is located. If their business needs a license, complain to the state agency licensing that business, such as the state bar or contractor's agency.
8. List bad clients and customers with an online service that lists fraudsters, such as Fraud Report (www.fraudreport.com). You can also tip off the FBI, Secret Service, and police fraud units. Though they are apt to consider this initially as a civil case, as reports mount up, these agencies may turn this into a criminal matter.
9. For an ongoing project, talk to the client or customer from time to time by phone or e-mail to reconfirm that you will charge for additional work and send ongoing bills.
10. Get the client or customer to confirm in writing any request for additional work and the expected charges.

11. Be alert for any signs of customer or client problems, such as indications of financial difficulties or the client changing his mind or abandoning the project.

In short, you may not be able to prevent all frauds by determined and resourceful con artists or client and customer fraudsters. But you can reduce the likelihood that they will successfully defraud you.

No matter what side you are on in a credit card transaction—whether as a consumer or client or as a merchant, professional, or freelancer—there are steps you can take to protect yourself from con artists, false charges, and overcharges and from fraud by clients and consumers. This book provides a detailed look at common credit card scams and offers practices that will help you better protect yourself in advance as well as deal with any problems that develop after a transaction that goes bad.

—Gini Graham Scott (adapted from an article that appeared as a *Huffington Post* blog on August 13, 2015)

INTRODUCTION

Everyone is affected by credit card fraud, and even the new chip cards can't fix most of this. That's because so much business today occurs over the Internet or via phone where no card is present. And fraudsters can get your card information in many other ways. But fraudsters do not only steal and use the credit card information of consumers; they also pose as complaining consumers to fraudulently get out of paying merchants for purchases made on a credit card.

Often these frauds occur due to identity theft or bogus online offers for products or services that aren't delivered or aren't as advertised. Another common fraud is "free trials" that turn out not to be free and become a nightmare of recurring charges after consumers unwittingly agree to a monthly charge for a membership to receive a product they don't want each month. Such scams entrap millions of consumers, and often law enforcement can do little, since there are so many fraudsters operating, many of them overseas. However, if consumers recognize and respond to the fraud in time, they can go to their bank, claim fraud, and get their charges reversed, usually with no dispute raised by the fraudsters, who are on to the next victim.

At the same time, due to tightening policies to protect consumers who claim fraud, another type of fraud that has gotten little attention is clients and consumers who are defrauding merchants, service providers, professionals, and freelancers by falsely claiming they have been defrauded and use their claim to get out of paying for a product or service. This scam is particularly a problem for those engaging in online transactions and getting paid by credit cards or PayPal, because when a client or consumer claims fraud, the merchant or other provider has to prove there was no fraud. Even extensive e-mail exchanges showing there was an authorized transaction aren't enough. Commonly, the online vendor also needs to show a contract or agreement for the product or service provided, plus other evidence showing that the client or consumer approved the transaction, willingly provided the card number, and actually received the product or service. But if the client or consumer says he or she didn't provide the number or didn't receive the product or service, that's usually it. It's like a person calling out "Fire" in a crowded theater, whereupon everyone flees, and when the authorities show there was no fire, the person who called out "Fire" gets away with no penalty for a false claim.

The problem is that clients and customers can easily lie to claim the charge wasn't authorized and that they didn't engage in the transaction. Normally this fraud claim doesn't happen with legitimate customers and clients, especially when there is an ongoing relationship. But some fraudsters use the crackdown on fraudulent credit card charges to pose as victims in order to defraud legitimate businesses that provide products or services via the Internet or phone. This situation has become increasingly common, as millions of vendors now use websites and customer service portals to attract customers and clients. Unfortunately, many of these vendors and service providers can be defrauded by credit card con artists.

Certainly, the vast majority of transactions occur without a problem, and many successful businesses have been built based on online and phone agreements and charges. Likewise, most customers and clients pay for and receive products and services via the phone or Internet without needing to have a face-to-face meeting. But the potential for fraud by clients, customers, and merchants alike is there.

In some cases, these transactions start out as legitimate purchases, such as when a client hires a writer or artist to do some work. But after the work is done, the client decides he wanted something else, while asking the writer or artist to keep working on the project. Or in some cases, the client decides to abandon the project entirely. Or perhaps the client has financial difficulties, making it difficult to pay, or worse, the client might seek to get back the money that was originally authorized and charged by claiming fraud. This fraud claim is like the guy claiming fire, since no one takes the time to check if there really is a fire. The merchant, service provider, professional, or freelancer consequently not only loses the payment for the products supplied or work done, but in addition, the fraud claim goes on his or her record. With enough of these fraudulent claims, vendors can lose their merchant account, seriously undermining their ability to conduct an online business in the future, which is based on obtaining credit card payments.

Conversely, sometimes what starts as a seemingly legitimate purchase can turn into fraudulent charges—or worse, a physical confrontation, when a criminal steals a credit card from a consumer and uses it to obtain a product or service. Sometimes consumers may find their credit hopelessly compromised, such as when a stolen credit card results in phony charges on their account. They may even be charged with a crime due to a fraudster using their credit card to engage in grand theft.

The Complete Guide to Preventing Credit Card Fraud is designed to help you do just what the title says, whether you are a consumer, client, merchant, service provider, professional, or freelancers, and to help you know what to do if you are victimized. While it may not be possible to protect yourself against all fraudsters, the tips and techniques in this book will help to prevent many fraudsters from taking advantage of you as both a consumer and merchant/provider. The book also offers guidelines that will help you create a trail of documents so you can defend yourself successfully against a fraudulent claim or charges should a fraudster steal your identity. This book will also teach you how to best respond to increase your chances of winning a dispute and exposing the scammers so they can't prey on others.

Included are chapters on the following topics:

- protecting your computer against fraudsters stealing your credit card data
- avoiding common consumer frauds based on using free trials to charge you for phony products
- securing your credit card information, from your mailbox to making purchases
- getting your money back after you have been scammed
- setting up a payment system to encourage payments from cash, money order, cashier's checks, cash, and direct bank deposits

- creating a merchant account, and setting up a verified credit card order form on your website
- obtaining agreements and contracts from clients for your products and services
- obtaining complete credit card information to show authorization
- documenting your e-mail and mail exchanges
- staying in contact with your customer or client to confirm arrangements and payments
- recognizing signs of customer or client problems, such as financial problems, changing what was originally asked for, or abandoning the project
- responding to a claim of fraud and nonreceipt of products or services by a client or customer
- keeping your account current in case of moves or changes in your business
- reporting the fraud to the appropriate agencies and reporting services

By drawing on the stories of individual consumers, merchants, service providers, professionals, and freelancers who have been scammed, along with providing a detailed discussion of the current laws and practices governing the use of credit cards, this book clearly outlines the dangers and offers essential advice to anyone participating in credit card purchases either as a seller or buyer.

Part I

Protecting Yourself as a Consumer or Client

I

PROTECTING YOURSELF FROM CREDIT CARD FRAUD AS A CONSUMER

Knowing how to be protected from credit card fraud is important for everyone, since business owners are vulnerable as well as consumers. The fraudsters just need a credit card number, name, and address or security code, and they can readily use it by pretending to be the credit card owner. They can get this information in various ways—from stealing your card, photographing or watching you while you use it, or engaging in some scheme to get you to reveal your number and identifying information. With this information, they can readily use your card online to get information, merchandise, or subscriptions, and use that to gain access to your private information. They can then use that information to defraud merchants by claiming the merchant defrauded them in some way, such as not delivering the merchandise in good working order at all or claiming that the order was made without their participation or authorization. The merchant usually will lose to any fraud claim, so the fraudster can easily turn merchants into victims while they are victimizing you.

So what can you do to protect yourself as a consumer?

THE RISK OF CREDIT CARD FRAUD

The likelihood of becoming a victim of credit fraud as a consumer or vendor is huge because the possible payout to the credit card scammers is so large and there are so many thousands of them, many in other countries. For most of these cases, you file a police report and an insurance claim; make a report to your credit card provider, PayPal, or bank; and then wait as these reports and claims are processed. Your case gets added to the stats, you eventually get reversed after two or three months, and you get your money back, but in the meantime, you have the hassle of having to deal with reporting the fraud or making a claim and perhaps having some economic distress when your money is tied up in the claims process before you get it back.

According to a 2014 *Economist* article, "Skimming Off the Top," the total global payout for credit card fraud losses was $11.3 billion in 2012, up 15 percent from 2011.[1] And in 2014, this number was even higher— a $16 billion global industry involved in credit card fraud around the world.[2] Moreover, the problem was even greater for consumers in the United States, the one country where counterfeit card fraud is consistently growing—it accounted for 47 percent of all types of fraudulent payment-card debt, according to the Nilson Report. The other big losers were card issuers, who lost $3.4 billion that year, while merchants lost another $1.9 billion.[3]

If you haven't yet been a credit card fraud victim, you might well be in the future, as researchers at the Aite Group, a research firm, and at ACI Worldwide, a payment-software firm, found in a 2012 survey that 42 percent of Americans had been victimized by some type of payment-card fraud in the past five years. One reason there is so much fraud is that the United States has more credit cards than other countries. As of the end of 2013, Americans had 1.2 billion debit, credit, and prepaid cards, with each adult having an average of five cards each.[4] And on average, individuals in high-income households have even more.

THE DIFFERENT WAYS YOU CAN BE VICTIMIZED

There are a number of ways you can end up being a victim in a variety of scams. They vary in the specific way they are conducted, but they all end up with the common result—the fraudsters get your physical cards or enough information about your card and you that they can use it to charge purchases or siphon money from your bank. Or they may get you to make a purchase, where you give up card information, and then they charge you and charge you for ongoing purchases or for more time on a subscription that you find it difficult to cancel. The scenario they use to get your card and information or entice you to buy something may differ—but the outcome is the same. You lose money. And so does the vendor, because it's a phony charge. Plus, there may be more losses, depending on the scenario that leads you to use your credit card or give the fraudster your information. A first step to protecting yourself is to become aware of the different strategies the fraudsters use, so you can become suspicious when a person seems to be using these strategies on you. And depending on circumstances, you can seek more information to see if your suspicions are confirmed or if the person is legit, you can walk away and not risk getting involved, or you can report the possible fraudster to the police if this is a local fraudster.

Some of the ways fraudsters can get your card or information about it are the following:

1. The fraudster uses a skimmer to collect information from an ATM, gas pump, or other place where you use a card.
2. The fraudster has set up a camera to take a photo of you using your card, and other identifying information about who you are, such as your license plate number.
3. The fraudster steals a card mailed to you from your mailbox and then activates that card.
4. The fraudster gets your card by stealing your wallet from your car, purse, jacket pocket, or other places where you might keep your card—or possibly obtains it in the course of a robbery.
5. The fraudster gets your card when you give it to a waiter or clerk at a restaurant, supermarket, or other retail establishment, makes a copy of it, and gives it back to you.
6. The fraudster uses a scam online to get you to give up your information, such as using a pretext of being from your bank, e-mail provider, or government agency verifying information from you.
7. The fraudster uses a phone call to get information from you, variously providing a sales offering, investment opportunity, or other reason for you to give up your credit card information.
8. The fraudster offers a product or service, possibly with a free trial, where you have to put in your credit card information, after

which you get charged not only for that product or service, which turns out to cost more than expected or to be an inferior product or service, but then the fraudster has your credit card information for use in the future.

9. The fraudster has a repair scam, especially for an auto or for your house or garden, where the fraudster not only gets money for work that isn't done or is not done well, but then has your credit card information for use in the future.

10. The fraudster involves you in an investment scam, where you use a credit card rather than a check to buy shares, and then not only can the fraudster provide you with worthless shares, but he or she can also use your credit card in the future.

11. The fraudster is able to hack into a retailer or other organization that has your credit card and personal information stores in the system.

12. The fraudster uses personal information about you to obtain credit cards in your name and then uses these to make other purchases or obtain loans, but not repay them.

13. The fraudster puts on a free event, advertises it heavily, and then does an effective sales pitch at the event, after which he or she gets credit card information to charge for future events or programs, which turn out to be of less value than promised or don't occur at all.

14. The fraudster sells your card or information about it to other fraudsters who are part of a network of credit card scammers.

However the fraudster gets your card or information about your card, he or she can then use it directly, usually for at least a day or two, until you discover the fraud and report it, thereby putting your card number on fraud alert. Then, the card can't be used again without you (or someone posing as you) calling the bank or card company to verify the user really is you with a number of questions. But if the fraudster has already collected information about you, that could be enough for the fraudster or an associate to get through this credit card screening.

So what can you do? Future chapters will describe individual scams and what you can do at more length. Here are some general principles to keep in mind to reduce your potential for being scammed and reduce your possible losses if you become a victim.

1. Don't carry all your credit cards in one place, so someone can't steal all of them at one time.
2. Don't leave your wallet, purse, or anything else with your credit cards in an insecure place, where it can be easily stolen or copied, such as in a room for coats and purses at a party or in your car's glove compartment.
3. Don't let anyone get too close to you at an ATM, gas station, or anywhere else where you put in your credit card to get money or make a purchase.
4. Notice if there are any cameras around that might be recording a video of you with your card making a payment, and consider the possibility that a camera might be recording your card, even if you can't see it. To avoid your card being photographed, cover it with your hand as you put it in to pay.
5. Avoid meeting advertisers selling goods or services in a private place or at the person's home or office, if this is a private party or new business, and meet in a public place so you can check that the person is who he/she claims to be, since there have been cases where people answered ads and got robbed.
6. Be cautious about free trial or lowball price offers on the Internet, since many companies that will run up unexpected high charges and fraudulent charges start with such an offer.
7. Check out the bona fides for any individual or company before you make a significant purchase or investment to see if what they are offering is real.
8. Check your bank statement online regularly, and report any unexplained charges on your statement immediately.
9. Get one of the new chip cards and use that rather than a card with a magnetic strip, since these are harder for fraudsters to use.
10. Make a copy of all your credit cards, so you can quickly report them if they are stolen; perhaps sign up with a service that reports any losses, since it will be faster to have someone do it for you.
11. Keep a low balance on your credit cards, and, since your debit card goes right to your bank, keep a low balance in whatever account is linked to your account. If you have a choice of what cards to use, use a credit card rather than a debit card, since that

will give you a day or two of insulation before being charged to your bank.

12. Use one of the alternate payment services, such as PayPal, when you can, since this will not reveal your credit card information when you make a purchase—and keep your user name and password as confidential as you can, to keep someone from using your PayPal account and using that to get your name, bank account, and other information.

13. As best you can, deal with established merchants in stores and online, or carefully check out anyone new by checking out their literature, looking at their website, and getting references from others who have bought from them or used their service, which will help to show if the seller is really sincere.

14. If you have been victimized, gather as much information as you can about your fraudster and what happened; and use this to inform the local police, sheriff, or other authorities; and tell your insurance company what happened.

15. Check with your insurance agency to be sure you are properly covered in case of a significant loss due to credit card fraud.

16. Change your credit cards from time to time and request a new one, which will probably be one of the new chip cards, which have more consumer protections.

You will likely think of other protective strategies. One key is to do what you can to keep your credit/debit card and information about you and your card safe and secure so fraudsters can't use it. The next key is to avoid scams to get information about your card and you as best you can. If you do feel you have been victimized, gather as much information about what happened and what you know about the fraudster and contact the police if the fraud happened in your area; otherwise, contact the FBI's Internet Crimes Unit. Also, contact your insurance company if the amount is large enough to make a claim.

The next chapters will describe the various scams and discuss what to do about each one in more detail.

2

DON'T GET SKIMMED—AND USING THE NEW CHIP CARDS

One of the sneakiest ways that credit card scammers can get your card information is through skimming, where a card reader harvests the data from your card's magnetic strip. A related method is for someone working at a retail establishment to copy the information on your card or take a quick photo of it. In either case, once obtained, your information can be used to make purchases—often online. The information also may be used to manufacture a card that looks legit. You may not even know you've been skimmed if you make a series of purchases with your card in one day. And since skimmers can easily move their equipment, when you report your suspicion that you have been skimmed, the authorities may not even be able to determine where the skimming happened, much less who did it.

HOW A CARD READER SKIMMER WORKS

A device that skims the information from credit cards may be incorporated into a legitimate card reader. Alternatively, it may be a separate device in which a salesperson in on the fraud, usually getting a commission of about $10–$50 for each card skimmed, secretly swipes the card a second time before returning the card to you. The swipe in the skimming device records details about the card, including the security code number on the back and any company name information on the front.

The magnetic strip includes the same basic information available on the card itself, including the cardholder's name, account number, expiration date, and the Card Security Code, also called the Card Verification Code or CVV. But now the fraudster has all this information without having to steal your actual card, which makes it possible to get more information about you from other sources. For example, if your address or other information is accessible elsewhere, such as on your social media account or website, a fraudster can readily use this information to make purchases without having your card or use this information to correspond to other personal identity you have in other databases and thereby open up other sources of data about you.

These skimming devices are small electronic magnetic readers that can be plugged into an ATM or gas pump very quickly. They look like a computer chip and ribbon, and they are able to access the ATM or gas pump system to scan the information encoded on the magnetic strip of credit or debit cards. The device is difficult to detect because it is very small and inside the machine, though a loose or jiggly front panel could suggest that someone has inserted one of these devices. According to the police, it takes only about thirty seconds for a criminal to install a device. They often just unlock the pump or ATM with a key. Sometimes they are able to get a manufactured key or get one copied, or they work out a commission arrangement with the ATM operator or someone at the gas station where the gas pump is located. They then attach the device inside so when you swipe your card it captures your information. Some skimmers have also become adept at prying open these machines. Thieves can use the skimmed information to clone your account by printing up new cards, which they can use to charge purchases until you report the fraud.[1] Often skimmers work as part of a cloning ring, where they provide the skimmed information to the ring members who do the cloning. Your cloned card may be used by the ring or sold to other criminals.

Because the skimming devices can't read the card's PIN, the fraudsters use cameras to capture the customer entering the number on the keypad. The cameras are the weakest link in the scheme, since they are the most likely element to give the scammers away. Typically, the fraudsters use very small battery-powered cameras mounted inside a light fixture already in place above an ATM keypad. Such a camera can see the card reader through a pin-sized hole and can be powered by a battery of only about three volts, which is the size of a small coin, so it can easily be placed on the thin metal platform that holds the camera. Usually the fraudster places the camera on the ceiling above the ATM, using double-sided tape. So the whole contraption might look like an upside-down beetle. If you see any strips on the top of the ATM or on a gas station canopy over the gas pumps, that could be a giveaway that your card is on candid camera, and you should report it—though not to the store owner or station attendant if you suspect that person might be in on the scam. Instead, contact your local police of sheriff's department.

Once a skimmer is in place, the fraudsters don't even have to come back to the location or hire someone inside the store, gas station, or other establishment to assist with obtaining the information collected on these skimmers. Instead, fraudsters can use a skimmer with wireless capabilities. So after installing the equipment, the fraudster can pick up the information on a smartphone from two hundred feet away, and might possibly use more sophisticated equipment to access the smartphone remotely from anywhere, much like a computer professional can use software to remotely view and take over your phone.

However, the fraudsters do need to return to get information from the cameras, because they can't store data for more than a few hours, and their batteries run out of juice quickly, since these cameras aren't able to stop and start filming on their own. The fraudsters or an associate therefore has to return to put in new batteries and SD cards. So if you see someone changing batteries, that's a time to be suspicious and notify someone—if not the store owner or gas station attendant, then law enforcement—and let them take it from there. Don't try to confront anyone yourself. Any local activity is part of a multimillion-dollar or even billion-dollar larger industry, so any confrontation could be dangerous or deadly.

While a PIN isn't commonly used on credit cards, it is on debit cards, and this can be obtained by a hidden camera, by a pressure-sensitive pad inserted underneath the keypad, or by someone behind the counter watching while you key in your PIN. Some fraudsters might also use a thermal imager for a smartphone, such as made by FLIR One, which can pick up the thermal images left behind on the number keys you just tapped to put in your pin. Of course, one way to evade such a technique to obtain your PIN is to place your fingers lightly on a few other keys without pressing them so it isn't clear which number you have pressed. Also, this approach can defeat a sensor that is picking up the heat of your fingers on the keys.[2]

Unfortunately, once a fraudster has obtained the information from a skimmer or other method of acquiring your card information, the fraudster can imprint that information onto a card that looks legitimate and key in your PIN. Then, the fraudster—or anyone who purchases the phony card—can simply go to an ATM or use the card for an in-store purchase. And then, until your card is on a fraud alert, it's open season for making purchases on your number.

While many of these skimming scams occur when you make a purchase at gas stations, convenience stores, and other retail establishments with card readers, they also occur at the ATMs located in bank branches and at convenience and other retail stores where you use your card to get cash. It's a fraud that has been growing, especially at ATMs located away from banks. For example, according to a *Forbes* article: "5 Ways to Protect Yourself Against Debit Card Fraud," by Nick Clemente, FICO reported in May 2015 that debit card fraud hit a twenty-year high, and fraud at ATMs in bank branches was up 174 percent from January 1 to April 9 in 2015 compared to 2014. And this increase was nearly twice as much for ATM machines located away from bank premises—up 317 percent.[3] A major reason for this big increase away from bank locations is that it is much easier for fraudsters to attach their skimming equipment there than in the ATMs at bank branches. Generally, the biggest risk is using an ATM machine that is outside the bank and using it after office hours, whereas you are usually safe using an ATM inside a bank lobby. In some cases, when you use an ATM after office hours, you commonly have to put your card in a reader to unlock the door—but this door can also be a good site for fraudsters to put a skimming device. So it is best to avoid ATM machines that are outside a bank branch. Rather, it is best to use an ATM at a bank branch during business hours if you don't want to wait for a teller to get cash, and avoid putting your card in a device that opens up the door to a bank after hours. Alternatively, if this option is available, rather than using a debit card to gain entry, use any other nonidentifiable card with a magnetic strip, such as a gift card from Starbucks or other merchant, which banks with indoor ATMS commonly allow to get inside.

Of course, in such a situation, if you quickly report it, you are likely to get all your money from your bank or credit card company in a couple of weeks. But in the meantime, the fraudster and others in on the scam can enjoy whatever they have illegally purchased with your stolen card information.

One way to spot a skimmer is if the card reader seems a little loose or seems to jiggle more than usual, which is a sign it may have been tampered with.[4] If you do suspect there might be a skimmer on the card reader, you might be better off paying inside, although the sales clerk might be in on the fraud and getting a commission on each sale processed through the skimmer or otherwise pulling information from it.

Some corporations have been proactive in addressing this problem through more security checks, though this isn't completely foolproof if any employee is part of one of these skimming operations. In this case, as Fountain reports, many corporate-owned gas stations have instituted a new policy whereby their employees are required to conduct inspections during every shift to check for skimming or camera equipment on or by any ATMs or gas pumps. And these corporations have active training programs to let employees know what to watch for. For instance, in San Luis Obispo, Detective Eric Vitale with the police fraud unit has been meeting with every gas station owner in the city to teach them how to detect machine tampering, so now nearly all of them routinely check their machines. Fuel pump manufacturers have also improved their products by making the keys used to open these pumps much harder to copy.

THE EXTRA SECURITY IN THE NEW CHIP AND PIN CARDS

While the newer chip and PIN cards are designed to avoid the problems of skimming, a problem is that these chip cards are still only accepted by a minority of businesses in America, though they are more widely accepted abroad. According to a March 6, 2016, CNBC article, "No Chips: A Slow Go for New Credit Card Technology," only 37 percent of American businesses can accept chip-enabled credit and debit cards, according to a survey by the Strawhecker Group. They conducted the survey of ninety-two payment service providers serving over 3.9 million merchants, representing about half of the retailers who accept cards. Supposedly, retailers, credit card companies, and merchants were supposed to adopt this new technology by October 1, 2015, or become liable for fraudulent transactions. But the acceptance of this new processing technology has been delayed because of technical problems, such as making the payment processor or gateway ready and not having enough technical staff available to implement the transition. Thus, very often, even if you have a new chip card, the merchant will ask you to swipe the card through the regular magnetic strip reader. If so, you are subject to the same risk of skimming as using an older magnetic-strip card. So use a chip card when you can, since these EMV (Europay, MasterCard, and Visa) cards use an embedded microchip to provide extra data protection when they are inserted into a chip card reader. They are more secure because each card produces a unique code for each transaction, so they can't be readily recopied through skimming like the magnetic strip cards.

On the other hand, it may be that some fraudsters are also set up to break through the security on the new chip cards. Therefore, it may be that they are just as insecure as any regular credit card. For example, on March 9, 2016, one couple in North Fargo, North Dakota, got a new chip debit card in the mail, along with bank literature on why they should activate and use their new card. But days after they received and activated the card, someone accessed their card information to purchase hundreds of dollars worth of merchandise at a local Walmart. When they looked more closely at their online checking account figures, they found a few dollars charged at a gas station they don't normally go to and two more purchases made minutes apart at their local Walmart. So it seems someone accessed their card information at Walmart, somehow cloned the card to be able to readily use it in other card readers, and then used the card to buy gas for their getaway.

Ultimately, the couple did get back their money from the bank once they reported the claim, and, intriguingly, while they were at their bank to get a new temporary card, another person came in with the same problem—someone using their new chip card—or possibly a clone of it—to commit a fraud online. So if this is happening when the new chip cards that are supposed to be more secure are first coming out, just think how that security might likely be easily breached again. If the fraudsters have found a way to access these secure cards, that makes the problem even worse, since people will be using these cards mistakenly thinking they are more secure and may be less alert when they use their card, especially if they put it through a card reader.

THE ADVANTAGES OF A CREDIT CARD VS. A DEBIT CARD

The difference between a credit card and a debit card is that a credit card creates a loan of credit to you, which you have to either pay off at the end of the billing period at no charge or pay a smaller amount monthly with interest added to the card. By contrast, the debit card takes the money directly from your bank account, and you have to have a PIN number for it. Only some of the new chip credit cards use a PIN. However, many debit cards can be used like credit cards, where you don't need a PIN, but the money still comes directly out of your bank.

Given the way these cards operate, you have more protection with a credit card, since the money doesn't come out of your bank right away. Instead, the balance builds up, and if you dispute the fraudulent use of your card, you generally will not be held responsible for those charges. By contrast, with a debit card, even though you may eventually get your money back, the consequences of fraud are more dire. First, since the money comes directly out of your account, the fraudster could take all of the money out of your account and might even take more, so you end up with a negative balance.[5] Meanwhile, in the time it takes to report and process your fraud claim and get a refund, other checks could bounce, racking up check bouncing charges. And if you have overdraft protection, the bank could take money out of another account to cover the excess charges, plus there will be an overdraft fee charge. In short, you could be facing a major mess at your bank because the skimmer has skimmed out much or all of your money. And even if the amount the fraudster charged is refunded, you still will commonly be stuck with the bounced check and overdraft fee charges.

THE COST OF SKIMMING AND THE DIFFICULTIES FOR LAW ENFORCEMENT

Skimming devices have actually been used by criminals dating back to about 2010, although they have become more and more popular for criminals and costly for consumers in the last few years. It is very difficult for law enforcement to combat this kind of rip-off. According to Matt Fountain, writing for the *Tribune* in San Luis Obispo, California, skimming investigations are considered "cop kryptonite," because they "require a lot of technical know-how and time, often with little payoff."[6] In the event the criminals are actually caught and tried or plead guilty, they serve little jail or prison time and often are out on the street in a short time, where, naturally, they continue to skim more victims.

Some of these skimming operations are really quite extensive—essentially a modern form of organized crime. For example, the FBI characterizes skimming devices as the "calling cards of Eurasian organized crime groups with associates born in or with family in Russia or Eastern Europe," and so far, the FBI has disrupted sophisticated organizations in Miami, Atlanta, Chicago, and New York. California was also very hard hit by a rash of skimming cases dating back to 2012, leading the state Department of Justice to launch a crackdown on these devices, using its eCrime Unit to prosecute the criminals in county-level superior courts.[7]

Law enforcement has also found that the groups installing these skimmers tend to target smaller communities, since the authorities generally know less about how to deal with them. In turn, the professional skimming groups are able to fund a lavish lifestyle with the money they make through fraud—and if anyone in their organization gets caught, they usually can have top lawyers represent them, since they have the money to pay for this. In fact, they tend to regard dealing with the police and responding to any busts as the cost of doing business. As one detective from San Luis Obispo, Detective Eric Vitale, noted, these can be very large organizations with different crews doing different activities, such as one crew to install the skimmers; another to harvest the information; a third to develop clones; another team to cash out by making purchases, obtaining money from the ATMs, and selling the clones to individual criminals or gangs; and a fifth group to launder the money. While the police can spend hours or days to find the lower-level skimmers who are installing the equipment by observing ATMs or gas stations and making arrests, their goal is to go up the organizational chain by tracking the skimmers to where the clones are being made.

HOW THE POLICE HAVE CAUGHT SOME SKIMMERS

While it can be difficult for the police to catch the skimmers who are placing the equipment on gas pumps and ATMs and then find the other gang members, they can better respond when they get leads from store-owners or residents who see suspicious activity. Then, once the police start cracking down in one area, the skimmers get the message and pursue skimming somewhere else.[8]

As an example, the San Luis Obispo police cracked a series of cases from 2010 to 2014, going from skimmers to the operators of a fraud ring. In 2010, the police got a call from employees at the Arroyo Grande RadioShack that three men attempted to use fake credit cards in the store. After the clerk told them they couldn't use their cards, they raced outside, jumped in a black Dodge Caravan, and drove off. Suspecting that the men might try to go to a RadioShack in San Luis Obispo—a stupid move since their cover was blown—the detectives headed to that store, and when they got there, they found one man still in the store, while the other two were in the parking lot.

After further checking, the detectives found that the men were each from the L.A. area and that they had a number of counterfeit credit cards with fraudulent names from three major financial institutions— Chase, Wells Fargo, and Capital One. In searching their car, the detectives found extensive paraphernalia showing their involvement in credit card fraud—among other things, the detectives found three gas pump skimming devices, plus fifteen gas pump keys, enabling them to open up the pumps and put in the fraudulent cards.

In a 2011 case, detectives arrested three Southern California residents for running a skimming operation based on credit card information they obtained from Chase Bank customers in San Luis Obispo for about $58,000. Then, in 2012, state prosecutors obtained convictions for three men who also targeted Chase Bank customers. They convicted them for making phone debit cards after using ATM card readers to obtain credit card information and cameras to capture PINs. They had fleeced about three hundred victims in Santa Clara, Marin, Fresno, and San Luis Obispo counties of about $220,000.

In 2014, Citibank customers at branches around Los Angeles County became the victims, and this time, the police arrested three Los Angeles–area residents in Paso Robles for operating a credit card fraud ring. In this case, the fraudsters used the cards to withdraw the money from customers' accounts, and the police found forty-six credit cards that they had created with real customer account information on their magnetic strips, obtained through skimming.

SUMMING UP: SOME TIPS TO AVOID BEING SKIMMED

Here is some advice to keep your card safe from the skimmers—or at least reduce your chances of being skimmed:

- Cover your hand when entering your PIN so a camera or someone standing close behind you can't pick up the numbers.
- Avoid using freestanding ATMs, since these are the most likely to have skimming devices attached to them.
- When you use an ATM, notice if the card reader is loose and jiggle the card reader to see if there might be a skimming device placed over the real card reader; if you see anything that looks suspicious, don't use that ATM, and if you can, use an ATM in the bank, or report your suspicions to a banker.
- When using a gas pump, check for anything that looks suspicious, such as a loose card reader, and notice if the coded tape that seals the machine has any breaks. If anything seems suspicious, pay inside. You can use a credit card if you trust the attendant, such as if it is the owner or a longtime employee, and you can also report your suspicions. Otherwise, if you suspect the attendant might be in on it, use cash, and if necessary, buy only a small amount of gas or merchandise at this station and go to another station where everything seems legit.
- Notice the lights above an ATM or gas pump. If they are out, that could mean that someone put in a camera, though it could mean they are just negligent. If there is a camera, you can protect yourself by covering your card with your hand; but a camera might also

mean there is a skimmer, so proceed as noted above, where you suspect the worst.

- Use a chip card, which doesn't depend on reading a magnetic strip alone, and has additional security features, such as changing the numbers for each transaction.
- Use a credit card, rather than a debit card. Though you will get your money back for a fraud claim based a skimmed card, you will generally get your money back faster if you have used a credit card, because the card companies want you to be able to spend more money, though in both cases, banks have up to thirty days to refund your money. Moreover, if you use a credit card, the money is a loan, whereas a debit card draws the money directly from your bank, and with a debit card, you risk the fraudster emptying the money out of your account.
- If in doubt, preferably use cash.

3

WAYS TO GUARD YOUR PERSONAL FINANCIAL INFORMATION

Aside from protecting your card information from skimming, there are other steps you can take to guard your private information from being used to create a card or make purchases using your name. If someone does obtain and use your personal information, there are steps you can take to restore your credit and connections. Chapter 9 describes what to do in these cases.

Some of the steps to take to ensure that your personal information is not compromised include securing your mail, destroying receipts with account numbers on them, not giving information out over the phone to callers, monitoring your credit report, and carefully reviewing statements. Many of these tips come from the Federal Trade Commission (FTC), which provides information to consumers about credit card protections.

KEEPING YOUR PERSONAL INFORMATION SECURE OFFLINE

It seems almost quaint to talk about securing your personal information offline, since so much of everyone's life today is online. According to some reports, the average person spends about three to eight hours a day online, between smartphones and computers. And usually we think of people stealing information by hacking into a computer or using a pretext to get someone to click here or there or provide some security information in response to an e-mail request.

But there are many ways in which you are vulnerable to getting your personal and financial information taken offline, which can open the door to all sorts of credit card frauds based on using your information to pose as you. According to the FTC's Consumer Information site,[1] there are a number of steps you can take. Not everything you do is foolproof, since the fraudsters can come up with still other methods to get your information, such as blowing up a safe you have locked). But at least you will reduce your chances of having your information stolen.

Make a Copy of Your Personal and Financial Information

If your wallet where you keep this information is stolen or lost, it is best to have another copy. Be sure to store this information in a location separate from your original personal and financial information. Possibly create a list of all of the personal and financial information you have stored, and if you have any of this information password protected, keep a master list of these items and the passwords, but be very careful to not reveal any of this secret information. Keep any lists in a different place from your files of personal and financial information; you can further use coding to indicate what information is going where. Also, it goes without saying: keep both the personal and financial information and your lists indicating what you have in a password-protected secure location.

Keep Your Information in a Safe, Secure Place

At home, this can mean finding a place for safekeeping, such as putting the most important documents in a lockbox or safe with a combination. Another possibility might be putting these documents in a drawer with a lock on it; for even more protection use a heavy-gauge lock so it is hard to cut through. Or, even better, use a combination lock.

When you use any kind of lock, lockbox, or safe that requires a combination to open it, don't use a combination that is easy to guess or any kind of master password that you use for multiple services and activities, since a fraudster who obtains your password for a service or activity can easily try out that password on other sites. (For instance, if you belong to a gym, and set up a password for getting in, using your locker, and accessing certain equipment, don't use that same password for other clubs you join.) Also, don't use common passwords that are easy to guess, and don't keep your passwords near wherever you are putting your documents.

While it can be hard to remember which passwords you use for what, a good approach is to obtain an app for safely storing passwords. Look for recommendations or check with a computer-savvy person as to the best app to use. Alternatively, if you don't feel comfortable putting your passwords in an app, you might create a list or create and print out an Excel file or spreadsheet showing what these different passwords go to—but make sure to delete this file from your computer after you print it so it can't be accessed by a hacker. When you create this list, use initials or code words for what each password goes to so anyone else finding the list won't know what the passwords are for. Also, make a few copies of this list and keep them in different places so if someone does make off with your list, you will have another copy. (And in that case, change all of the passwords as soon as you can and make another list.) Consider changing your passwords regularly, too, and if you do, keep your lists updated and stored in different places that are secure.

One reason for all of this security at home is that sometimes burglars may not only be after cash or valuable property they can use or sell but also your personal information. They can then use it themselves or resell it to fraud rings that use it to access your bank account or create credit cards in your name. Thefts of information also sometimes occur when fraudsters pose as tradespeople such as plumbers, electricians, and painters and use their access to locate where your documents are so they can later come back and take them in what appears to be a regular burglary. Another scenario is if you hire people to work regularly in your home, such as a cleaning service or gardener, and they locate your personal documents and then arrange to return when you aren't there. Keep your information away from any roommates who share your house as well, and in the event of any kind of break-in or apparent theft or copying of your documents, change your passwords.

At work, some of these same rules apply, although you should take some time to think about your workplace and decide where it is most secure. For example, it might be safer to find a place apart from your own workspace for passwords, since if the fraudsters access this spot, they may not be able to relate it back to you. The information might belong to a number of people you work with. It's also good to have a multistep process for organizing and storing your information to keep it safe. For example, step one might be to collect all the information you need to protect. Step two might be to write down such things as stock numbers that might later be helpful to show the information you have collected and protected is assigned to you. Step three might be to obtain a heavy box or case to store this information, which ideally has a place to enter your protected password. And step four might be to determine where to store this box. In some cases, you might add it to an office safe that is open to all employees, or perhaps put the box in one of the drawers in your desk and then protect that with a sturdy lock.

Consider, too, the possibility of moving your stored documents around in case anyone at work has been observing where you keep this information. And, as at home, if you use passwords for anything, use different passwords for different activities, make a list of these passwords and what they go to using codes to obscure what goes with what, make several lists, and put them in a secure place.

Limit the Number of Cards You Carry with You

Ideally, just take the cards you need so if you lose your wallet or card case or it is stolen, there are fewer cards you have to replace and fewer cards crooks can use to get credit in your name or steal your identity.

The main cards to take with you when you go out are your driver's license or other identification card if you don't drive and preferably a single credit or debit card. If these cards are lost or stolen, you can readily cancel them and get others. Other cards to take with you are any shopping or activity cards for where you are going, although even if they have no personal information on them, they could still help to show your interests and memberships, which can help fraudsters present themselves as you, along with your personal information. You should leave your Social Security card at home, and instead of taking your Medicare or other medical insurance cards with you, which might be useful in the case of an emergency, take a copy with all but the last four numbers blacked out. Although if you are going to a doctor's office, take the original.

Limit the Information You Share with Others

You may be asked for personal information in a number of situations, such as when you get a job, enroll in school or enroll your child, or go to a doctor's office. As best you can, give out as little information as possible. To do so, ask the person requesting this information why they need it, how they will keep it safe from others, and what will happen if you don't share this information. In some cases, the requester may excuse you from providing the information on a form you are filling out, though in other cases, you may have to provide this information if you want the job, school enrollment, doctor's appointment, or other service. But at least you will know the reason for obtaining this information and how it will be safeguarded. You will then be better able to act in the event of a breach. For example, if the company you work for is suddenly hacked and your information is at risk, you can change passwords, change your bank account, and the like.

Shred Documents with Your Personal Information That You No Longer Need

You will find that all sorts of documents you don't need have your personal information on them, such as receipts, credit offers, credit applications, insurance forms, physician statements, checks, bank statements, and expired charge cards. When you throw them away, don't just put them in the trash as is. Some fraudsters use dumpster diving as a way to get personal information they can use for creating credit cards, dipping into bank accounts, and identity theft for other purposes. Instead, invest in a paper shredder to shred such documents, which will destroy the information. After all, unless you are very wealthy and involved in some serious litigation, no one will attempt to put all of the pieces of a shredded document together. The fraudsters will move on to easier targets.

Be Careful about Who Gets Your Health Information

In addition to shredding unneeded documents, you want to get rid of the labels on prescription bottles, since these also provide information about you that can be connected with other personal information. For instance, a prescription label will typically have your name and address as well as provide clues to any medical condition you might have. So destroy any labels on these bottles before you throw them out.

Also, be sure that you are sharing any health information only with legitimate providers. For example, don't share your health plan information with an individual offering free health services or products, since this could be a ploy to get your information to charge you later on for unneeded and unwanted products or services.

Protect Your Mail from Fraudsters Who Might Steal Your Mail

Another way that fraudsters can obtain personal information about you is from the mail you get. Increasingly, people are getting their mail online through e-mails. But there are still things you are likely to get or send in the mail rather than online, presumably for more security, such as checks, contracts, and official documents. Of course, a mail carrier or UPS driver might drop off packages for you when you aren't home and you haven't requested. So forgo the convenience of leaving outgoing mail in your mailbox and take it to a mailbox, post office, or a private mail and delivery service, such as a UPS Store. When you do get mail delivered to your house, take it out of your mailbox as soon as possible, since this will reduce the risk of a fraudster coming by to sweep it up as he or she makes the rounds of your neighborhood. If you won't be at home for several days, put in a request at the post office for a vacation hold. Plan your vacation hold so you can place it two or more days before you leave. Or perhaps for even more security, open up an account at a local mail service, which can receive and send your mail. If you go out of town, no worries. They will just gather up any mail that doesn't fit in your box, let you know you have mail, and you can pick up everything on your return.

Don't Have Any Important Documents Delivered to Your Home

Again, the reason for this is you don't want anything with your personal identifying information available so the fraudsters can pick these up from your mailbox. Thus, for example, if you order new checks or have signed a contract, don't have them sent to your home unless you have a secure mailbox with a lock on it. Or better yet, have these sent to the mail service that receives your mail.

Consider Opting Out of Prescreened Credit or Insurance Offers

These offers could provide you with some benefits if you are looking for more credit or want a better insurance deal than you have now. Companies will commonly send these to your home address, even if you use a mailing service—and you may get them there, too. However, if these come to your home mailbox, they will include your personal information, and they could even open up the door for a fraudster to seek credit in your name and ask for further communications to be sent to another address. So you may prefer to protect yourself from these offers rather than risk the misuse of your personal information. If so, you can opt out, according to the FTC's Consumer Information Unit by calling 1-888-567-8688 or go to optoutprescreen.com. You then indicate what address should be excluded from future mailings, and the credit companies and insurance companies should stop sending you these offers.

KEEPING YOUR PERSONAL INFORMATION SECURE ONLINE

Today it has become more and more difficult to keep your personal information online secure, because whatever you post or whatever anyone else posts about you can be fair game for anyone else to access or post. Even with certain privacy options in place, repeatedly there have been reports of breaches allowing fraudsters to access information, as well as repost it if there is a reason to do so—such as when a well-known person's information gets leaked. And then there are the hacks of databases, such as the theft of data from Target stores, the hack of Sony and the reposting of confidential e-mails from Sony officers, and even the compromised personnel data of the IRS.

So once anything is entered online—or you submit an application for a service that later is entered into a database—all of that is potentially open to access by others. And anything posted or stored in the cloud potentially can be discovered by sophisticated hackers or fraudsters who obtain the passwords, usually by tricking someone in the organization to give it to them. A recent example of this is the ersatz memo sent by a "CEO" of a company to payroll and HR officers to get PDFs of all the personnel records of employees. Well, some payroll and HR officers did just that, thinking this was an urgent memo from their CEO. Once the information was received, the fraudsters had employees' names, addresses, Social Security numbers, educational institutions attended, and more. So they could easily use that to get driver's licenses, passports, bank account access, and new credit cards, and so on. And often such fraudsters are in another country, most notably in Asia or Eastern Europe, making it very difficult for law enforcement to do anything about such online crimes.

Thus, while anything about you can potentially turn up online, putting you at risk of having your personal information stolen, at least you take some steps to reduce the risk. According to the FTC's Consumer Information site, here are some of the major things you can do.

Be Careful About Who Receives Your Personal Information

You have to be careful, because there are a lot of impersonators who may try to get information from you by calling you, sending you e-mails, inviting you to enter information on websites, or even sending you letters. They may give you various reasons for wanting this information, such as being with a government agency, wanting to inform you that you have won a prize in a lottery, having noticed problems with your bank account, or needing you to confirm your e-mail account. These are all various scams to get your personal information for various types of credit card fraud and stolen identity scams. So don't fall for them and give out your information or click on any links in the e-mail—the link might be a way of depositing a Trojan horse device on your computer that can gather your personal information, or in some cases could be ransomware, which deposits coding on your computer that locks it until you pay money—typically about $500–$1,000, or sometimes more—to get your computer unlocked. Then, too, a fraudster may pose as being someone you know or from an organization you know asking for information, and if they have communicated with you before, you may think this is a communication that is really from them. This is what is known as a "phishing" scam, where someone poses as someone else to fish for information from you. So don't fall for it. It's fine when you get regular communications from the person you know or your bank, insurance agent, or other company providing you with an update, such as when your bank lets you know your statement is available for viewing now. But be suspicious if this individual or company asks for personal information on line, since they will normally already have whatever information you have already given them, such as on a bank application to open an account. Requesting it online is often an information-gathering scam.

You can ignore these suspicious requests for information or check out the request before giving up any personal information. One way is put your mouse over the e-mail or any links in the e-mail, which will show the real e-mail address or URL of the person sending the e-mail. Alternatively, send an e-mail to the person you know who has contacted you (but type in the person's name into a new e-mail—don't hit reply, because that may go to the fraudster). Still another way to check is to type the company name into your Web browser, go to their site, and contact their customer service representative. Or call the company service number on your account statement. However you contact the individual or company, ask if the company really sent the request. Very often they will say they have not, and it's best to delete this e-mail, discard the letter, or don't return the suspicious phone call.

Be Careful When You Give Out Your Card at Restaurants and Retail Stores

One of the major ways that scammers can get your card information offline to either make purchases or use it for identity theft is when you give your card to a waiter at a restaurant or a clerk at a supermarket, gas station, or other retail store. Normally, this won't happen at a reputable company, but be aware that it can happen, and checking your online credit card or bank statement can help you notice if there is any unusual activity on your card. Then, not only can your card be stopped and replaced, but if you can track back to when you last used the card and the unauthorized charge appeared soon after that, then it can be easy to tie it to the place where it happened. But if the scammer waits a little longer before using the card—and the scammer can easily wait, since you have the card back from whatever you last purchased, it may be difficult for you to know exactly who committed the theft.

In any case, the thing to watch for is what happens after you give the person your card, if you can, to be sure someone doesn't take a picture of the card or otherwise record it other than on your credit card receipt.

Carefully Dispose of Any Personal Information—So You Really Get Rid of It

Whenever you are getting rid of anything with your personal information on it, such as your computer, smartphone, or other mobile device, permanently delete it so someone can't get this information from your equipment. For example, if you are getting rid of a computer, don't just delete information, since it will still be on your hard drive. Rather, reformat the whole drive, which eliminates any information on it, or use a wipe utility program that will overwrite the drive.

If you get rid of a smartphone or mobile device, check in your owner's manual or on the website of your service provider or the device manufacturer to see what they recommend to delete information permanently as well as how to save or transfer information to a new device. Among other things, remove the memory or SIM (subscriber identity module) card from the device. Also, take out your phone book, list of calls made and received, voicemails, and messages sent and received. Additionally, if you have any organizer folders, take those out, and delete your Web search history or any photos.

Encrypt Your Personal Information If You Send It Online

If you engage in any online transactions where you provide personal information, such as your credit card, debit card, bank account number, or password, keep your browser secure by using encryption software that scrambles any information you send over the Internet. You'll find dozens of encryption software products if you search online. For example, some of the most popular ones according to an encryption software review site[2] are FolderLock, SecureII, and Kruptos2. If you see a "lock" icon on your Internet browser's status bar, that means your information will be safe when you send it. So look for the lock before you send any personal or financial information online.

Use Strong Passwords and Keep Them Private

Be careful with your password, too. Your password safety starts with choosing a good one and from time to time changing it. Also, use different passwords for different sites, or at least for the sites that have your personal information and are most likely to be hacked, such as if you engage in online banking or access your health provider account online.

If you have a lot of e-mail, website, and social media accounts, it can be daunting if you need a password for each one. But there are a couple of work-arounds. One is to create a list all of your accounts and sites with passwords, such as in a typed and handwritten document that you don't save or post anywhere online to avoid someone hacking into your computer and obtaining all of this information. Then, when you change a password note this on the list.

Alternatively, you might use the same password for several accounts or sites that have a similar focus. For example, you might use one password for everything related to your passion for sports, another password for everything having to do with films, and so on. This way you have fewer passwords to remember and there is a logical connection between all the accounts or sites with the same password.

As for choosing the password, there are different schools of thoughts about that, with some people preferring a much harder to remember password composed of a mixture of lower- and uppercase letters, numbers, and symbols, with no repeating letters, such as DEH@xyr32!Frd. For others, a mix of upper- and lowercase letters, numbers, and perhaps just a comma somewhere might be fine, such as Deny,123, which has no repeating letters, but has a helpful reference to a name (Denny) with one "n," so it's easier to remember. Another possibility for creating a password is to substitute numbers for some words or letters, such as in this transformation where "I hope to visit Australia and New Zealand soon" might be encrypted as 1H2VAnzS.

Don't Post Too Much Information about Yourself on Social Media Sites

Be careful about what you post on the social media sites like Twitter, Facebook, LinkedIn, Instagram, and others. While you can limit access to your post as well as your site to a select group of people, there is always the risk that this information could still get out, say if someone forwards it on to someone outside the group or a hacker hacks their way into the site. So consider anything you post on these sites as potentially available to anyone, and know that it is likely to remain up there forever. The same caution applies to online forums, such as on websites or popular activity platforms like Meetup, when you post a profile. With the exception of the situation where you want people to know your name, company, occupation, and achievements, because you are promoting what you do to get clients, you should not post your full name, address, and phone number. And in no case should you post your Social Security number or account numbers on any site that is accessible to the public. The problem with posting too much information about yourself is that a fraudster can use the information about you to answer challenge questions on your accounts, such as "What is the name of your first pet?" and use this to get access to your financial and personal information. For those who are using their name for promoting their work, unfortunately, that is one of the risks that comes with getting known in this media age, and you have to take other steps to protect your accounts, such as setting up these accounts under another name, such as your full real name or creating a fictitious doing-business-as name in lieu of the first and last name you use in your business promotions.

Avoid Giving Permissions to Access Your Contacts and Personal Information

Another caution in using social media is to avoid responding to requests and offers that ask you to give permission to access your friends or e-mail list or that ask you to put in a lot of personal information about yourself. Often these take the form of quizzes that enable you to find out such things as your memory ability, dog that best suits your personality, or health age. While some of these are ways to troll for potential customers for a product or service, some may be attempts to gain more information about you and your contacts that could open the door to credit card fraud and identity theft. So check out who is asking for this information, and if in doubt, don't give your permission.

PROTECTING YOUR SOCIAL SECURITY NUMBER

Keeping your Social Security number confidential is especially vital to protecting yourself again credit card or identity fraud, since this number is like a door that opens up so much other information about you. You may have to let others know in a particular situation, such as in applying for or accepting a job, but you may be able to share it in a more secure way, such as faxing in an application form rather than e-mailing it. Then, too, if you send a form in an attachment rather than filling out an online form, this could provide another layer of protection, since fraudsters, like most criminals, want to take advantage of what information is most readily available to them, and opening up an attachment adds an additional step. In any case, the FTC's Consumer Information Unit recommends that you should ask questions before you decide to share that number for yourself or a child. For instance, ask if you can use a different kind of identification. You might also ask why they need your number, how they will use it, how they will protect it, and what will happen if you don't share that number.

Obviously, under certain circumstances, you may have no choice, such as when you are applying for a driver's license or working with a tax professional who is preparing your tax returns. As the FTC's Consumer Information Unit notes: "A business may not provide you with a service or benefit if you don't provide your number."[3] Also you will have to share your number with your employer and financial institutions, which need your SSN for wage and tax reporting purposes. And a business may ask for your SSN so they can check your credit when you apply for a loan, rent an apartment, or sign up for utility service. So there really are legitimate times when you do have to give out your information; just do what you can to keep down the exposure of your SSN beyond these required times, which will reduce the opportunities for a fraudster to access your credit or personal ID.

KEEPING YOUR DEVICES SECURE

Besides being cautious about how you give out information or share it, be careful to secure your devices so fraudsters can't access them. According to the FTC's Consumer Information Unit, there are five ways to do it, as described below.

Use Security Software

The goal here is to protect yourself against intrusions and infections that can corrupt or access your computer files or passwords. To this end, install antivirus and antispyware software and create a firewall. You can also install security patches on your operating system and other software programs. Some of the major vendors of this software include McAfee, Norton's Anti-Virus, and Trend Micro. Ask your computer or IT provider what to do, since this is probably not something that an average consumer knows about, and you don't want to screw up your computer by trying to do it yourself if you don't know what you are doing.

Avoid Phishing E-mails

As previously noted, a phishing e-mail is a pretext to start an exchange with you whereby you give up your credit card or other personal information. In addition, phishing e-mails can access your information when you open files, click on links, or download programs to learn more; once you do, you end up with a computer virus or spyware on your computer or smartphone that captures your passwords and any other information you type, or gains access to other files or e-mail records on your device. So if you don't know who sent something or don't expect whatever they sent, be very cautious, because the e-mail may be designed to get you to respond in some way that will at the very least show you have a good e-mail for a future correspondence. Don't open such files, click on links in the e-mail, or download programs sent by someone you don't know or is not what you expect from someone you know. It could well be a phishing expedition to lure you in and capture your information, like reeling in a fish on a line.

Be Careful When You Use Wi-Fi

Still another risk of revealing your personal information comes when you use a laptop or smartphone in a public place with a wireless network, such as a coffee shop, library, airport, or hotel.

While it can be inexpensive and convenient to take advantage of the free or cheap Wi-Fi available in such places, check if your information will be protected there. One source of protection might be if you have to get a password to access the Wi-Fi; another might be if the limited range of the Wi-Fi means that only those who are in the location can use the site, although be aware that another patron at the location might potentially be a fraudster collecting data from unsuspecting customers using the Wi-Fi at that location. However, if you use a secure wireless network, any information you send or receive on that network is protected. Also, be aware that if you go to an encrypted website, it will only protect the information you send to and from that site, but not other information.

In short, be aware that when you use Wi-Fi in a public place, you may expose your personal and financial information to others on that network, unless you have taken steps to secure your computer, laptop, or smart phone and are using encrypted data or an encrypted website.

Keep Your Laptop or Smartphone Locked Up

For further protection, lock up your laptop or smartphone and avoid putting financial or personal information on it if possible. This way you not only help to make it more secure from access over a wireless network but protect your data in case your laptop or smartphone is lost or stolen. Also, don't use an automatic login feature that saves your name and password, since that only provides an open season for any fraudster who steals or finds your device. And for the same reason, log off when you are finished with a session so someone else can't simply continue to use your device without logging in.

Check a Company's Privacy Policies to Make Sure You Are Comfortable with Them

This final FTC Consumer Information recommendation may or may not be useful, since not everyone has the time or interest in reading these long and complex descriptions of privacy policies that are posted online or are sent to you via e-mail or mail when you are considering opening up an account or doing business with a company online. Also, much of these policies is standard boilerplate that anyone has to agree to by checking a box where you say "I agree." However, many of these policies offer you options to have your information passed on to third parties to send you information, and you can always opt out. In essence, these privacy policies tell you "how the site maintains accuracy, access, security, and control of the personal information it collects; how it uses the information, and whether it provides information to third parties."[4] As the Consumer Information posting recommends: "If you don't see or understand a site's privacy policy, consider doing business elsewhere." Or you might limit how much information you provide, and sometimes you can reduce your exposure by providing an alternate e-mail or pen name that you use to protect yourself from that site getting more information about you or sharing it with others.

4

CREDIT CARD OFFERS

You may get all kinds of credit offers in the mail, via e-mail or by phone, for everything from a credit card with a lower interest rate to protection from credit card loss. You are especially likely to get such offers if you have had some credit card problems, such as going through a bankruptcy, and are trying to repair your credit. There are also credit repair companies that offer services to repair your credit. While some of these offers may be legit, they may also cost you money you don't need to spend, or you may find unexpected charges that are hidden in the small print. And some of these offers verge on or are outright scams. This chapter describes a number of these offers so you can evaluate them more critically, decide if you want to take them, and avoid the scams.

PRESCREENED CREDIT OFFERS

These are offers to get a credit card or get a card with a better rate. These are generally legitimate offers; however, many of them come with a catch that you may not be aware of—and if you get one of these cards, you may find you end up with poor customer service if you run into problems in getting a product or service and want a refund. Another problem may be a mix-up about whether your payment was received in time or whether you were sent a statement to make a pay-

ment, resulting in high interest charges and late fees, followed by problems dealing with customer service.

How a Prescreened or Preapproved Offer Works

These prescreened offers come from companies that are seeking new
credit card accounts, and they use prescreening to identify potential
customers for their cards. Sometimes these take the form of "preapproved" offers, meaning that you have met the initial criteria of the
company to receive the credit card. This offer doesn't guarantee you
will actually get the card, though perhaps 90 percent of the people
receiving these offers do qualify. Usually, you will get these offers in the
mail, though sometimes a company rep may send you an e-mail or call
you.

They get your name in one of two ways, according to the FTC's
Consumer Information Unit. One way is that the creditor sets its criteria, such as a minimum credit score, and it asks a consumer reporting
company for a list of people in the company's database who match this
criteria. Alternatively, the creditor will provide the consumer reporting
company with a list of potential customers and ask the company to
indicate which ones meet certain criteria. In either case, the offer goes
to those people who meet the criteria.

Commonly these offers go to people who need help in rebuilding
their credit, for example, after a bankruptcy or a period when they had
financial difficulties with a series of late or missed payments or they
acquired some collection accounts. The companies will often offer a
credit card with a low balance and allow the balance to increase after
the customer uses the card for six months to a year without missing
payments. Customers also may increase their credit score by just having
a credit card and making some regular payments. Even token payments
of perhaps $35 a month or less may be enough to establish a regular
payment record to increase their credit score. While many banks do
offer secured credit cards for people rebuilding credit, they typically
want a higher credit score—perhaps 680 or higher—to start with than
do banks offering these low-balance or secured cards for the subprime
credit market, which may contact you if you have a score of perhaps 550
or more. As you recover from a difficult financial period, your score will
creep up and you will start to get more and more offers. For example,

one person who got a series of offers from Capital One and a few other companies with $75 setup fees suddenly began getting offers from banks with only $35 setup fees.

The Problems with Prescreened and Preapproved Offers

While these cards do help some people increase their credit score, their score will go up naturally without these cards as time passes and no more credit inquiries occur. Additionally, many cardholders have had complaints about the extra charges on these cards, missed statements and poor customer service that result in more charges, and problems in getting refunds for returned purchases even when a retailer has processed a refund.

A key problem is that many of these card offers don't make it clear that customers will be charged a setup fee or monthly maintenance fee, and this charge is hidden in the fine print or at the end of the sales copy. In fact, this fee is deducted from the amount of credit offered, assuming the card is approved. For instance, a typical offer may provide a credit card with an initial balance of $500 to $700, but then $75 is deducted as the account setup fee, so the customer is only getting $425 or $625 credit to start. These offers typically come with an expiration date of fifteen to thirty days to inspire the customer to act quickly.

As an example, an offer for a credit card from the Merrick Bank, which specializes in subprime loans, provides this glowing sales copy for anyone seeking to "build or re-establish your credit." As the copy reads in part:

> Good News for [your name]
>
> **You have been pre-approved for the Double Your Line™ Visa© Credit Card with a $700 credit line!** Enjoy the advantages of a Visa credit card with no account set-up fee, no penalty rates, no "up to" credit lines . . . which means no surprises!
>
> **You can DOUBLE your $700 credit line to $1400** by making at least your minimum monthly payment on time for the first 7 months your account is open. After you make your payments, the increase is automatic . . .
>
> Don't wait—**This offer expires April 28, 2016**. . . . This is a terrific opportunity to help build or re-establish your credit!

And then a panel on the side repeats the main advantages of the account—no account set-up fee, no penalty rates, no over limit fee, monthly FICO Score for Free, $700 approved credit line, double your line to $1,400. However, buried in the "Summary of Terms" on the back, under "Fee," there is an annual fee of $36 for the first year, which is billed at $3 a month thereafter, plus $12 for each additional card, which is deducted from the $700, so the individual's initial credit is only $664, or $652 for an additional card. And then there are high charges for late payments or returned items of $37 for each time, and an especially high rate for cash advances—30.70 percent—and for interest at 25.70 percent, which could increase with an increase in the prime rate. Thus, the offer is not quite as good as it seems from the sales copy—which is characteristic of these prescreened and preapproval credit offers that come from banks or companies with merchant card arrangements for the subprime market.

SOME FTC WARNINGS ABOUT THESE PREAPPROVED OFFERS

The FTC itself urges consumers to be skeptical about preapproved card offers, which sometimes go by the name of gold or platinum card offers, that promise to get you a major credit card or improve your credit score. As the FTC points out, the marketers of these cards will often make a number of promises. For example, if you participate in their credit programs "you will get a major credit card (like an unsecured Visa or MasterCard), no-fee cash advances, lines of credit from national specialty and department stores, improve your credit rating, and other financial benefits." But, in fact, the real truth is very different—and you can do further research on complaints about a particular company making an offer through the FTC database[1] as well as with the Better Business Bureau if you do a search for the company name and the word "complaints." More specifically, the FTC warnings include the following:

Some marketers charge high fees for their cards without making it clear that the company will be charging those fees. Thus, you should read your credit card agreement carefully to be sure you understand all of the fees associated with your card.

While with some cards you can get lines of credit from national specialty and department stores, there is a big caveat with some cards. One is that your purchases may be limited to overpriced merchandise in specialized catalogs. Also, you may not be allowed to charge the total price of an item. Instead, you have to pay a cash deposit on each item you select—generally what the catalog company paid for the product. After you pay the deposit, you can charge the balance.

Although marketers claim you will improve your credit rating or get a major credit card as a result of signing up for one of these credit cards, this isn't true. Obtaining one of these cards almost never improves your credit rating or enables you to get a major card. Rather, the best way to improve your credit is to pay your bills on time. Moreover, your credit experiences may never get reported to the credit-reporting companies if the merchant you buy something from isn't a subscriber to these companies. So if a marketer claims that information about your experiences will be reported, call those companies to make sure that the merchant is in fact a member. If not, your experience will not be reported to help increase your score and the marketer has given you false information to get you to sign up for the program.

Commonly, you can only get a secured major credit card through these credit card offers. When you get a secured card, you typically have to place a security deposit ranging from a few hundred to several thousand dollars in a bank account. Then, your credit line is a percentage of the deposit—commonly 50–100 percent. However, you have to put up the funds before you get the card, and after that the company offering the card will check your credit. If you aren't approved for the card, you will get your deposit back, but you will have another inquiry on your credit report which could result in lowering your credit score by a few points. Moreover, even if you have shown a continuing pattern of regular payments following a difficult financial period with missed payments or a bankruptcy, a bank may deny you getting a card because the bank suffered a charge-off from you in the past. For example, one woman who had $10,000 in the bank and put up $300 for a secured credit card, which she wanted to rebuild her credit after a bankruptcy two years earlier, was turned down for a card because the bank had lost about $10,000 in a charge-off, even though she could clearly pay for any charges and the bank wouldn't suffer any risk, since it already had her money as a security. So be aware that a preapproved offer for a secured card may not be a sure thing—and the application could further reduce your credit score, making it harder to get another card when you apply again.

The advertising that you can use the card to get a no-fee cash advance can be misleading, since the free cash advance offer may actually be from an unrelated payday lender for a short-term, high-interest loan. But you can get this loan just by going to the payday lender directly and don't need to get the card.

PROBLEMS WITH SUBPRIME CREDIT CARD LENDERS

Although some individuals who have responded to these subprime credit card offers have successfully used these cards to reestablish credit, there have been a huge number of complaints, too, reported to various consumer watch groups, including the Consumerist (www. consumerist.com), Pissed Consumer (www.pissedconsumer.com), the Better Business Bureau (www.bbb.org), and RipOff Report (www. ripoffreport.com). While there have been complaints about the major credit card companies, including Amex, Bank of America, Citibank, Chase, and Wells Fargo, two of the top ten are Barclays and Capital One, according to the Consumerist,[2] and the Capital One cardholders filed the most disputes between September 2010 and November 2013—1,044 disputed claims, representing one out of five Cap One complaints. For the most part, these complaints were about billing issues (18 percent), high interest rates (10 percent), identity theft (7 percent), credit reporting (7 percent), and problems with closing or canceling accounts (6 percent), with most of the complaints (60 percent) resolved with an explanation from the card company. Only about 29 percent got monetary relief, and 10 percent of the cases got some sort of nonmonetary relief.

Yet, however the complaints were finally resolved, these represent only those filed with the Consumer Financial Protection Bureau (CFPB),[3] which began its credit card complaint portal in September 2010, resulting in more than 25,000 complaints, according to the January 2015 article in the Consumerist.[4] The CFPB was established by the Dodd-Frank Wall Street Reform and Consumer Protection Act of 2010 (Dodd-Frank Act), and in January of 2012, President Barack Obama appointed Rich Cordray to be its first director. Among other things, it supervises companies; enforces federal consumer financial protection laws; restricts unfair, deceptive, or abusive acts or practices; takes consumer complaints; promotes financial education; researches consumer behavior; and monitors financial markets for new risks to consumers.

Not all complaints are registered by this agency, however, in part because the agency is unfamiliar to many consumers, and there are hundreds of complaints on other sites, most of which appear to be unresolved, with little or no feedback from the companies complained about. Typical complaints are regarding overcharges, excessive interest payments, and problems with getting charged despite attempts to cancel the card. Some consumers report damage to their credit, although a major reason for consumers getting these cards in the first place is to repair or rebuild their credit. Following are samples from major complaint sites of complaints about three of the subprime banks that send these preapproved offerings—Merrick Bank, Barclays Bank, and Capital One.

For example, one pissed-off consumer from Ripon, California, on March 7, 2016, complained about Merrick's customer service generally:

> Merrick bank has the worst consumer service; I spoke with a rep named Jackie. . . . She provided horrible service. I then asked to speak to her supervisor and received even worse service!! They did not help me whatsoever, I am going to pay my account off and close this credit card. . . . Merrick prays on the consumer who does not know their rights as well as those who speak Spanish. . . . I am going to file a complaint with the Federal Trade Commission and encourage others to do the same.[5]

Another consumer from Marysville, Tennessee, complained on March 4, 2016, about getting hit with extra charges after not getting a statement, and the customer service people would do nothing to correct it. As the consumer complained:

> I just received my bill. It was really high, so I called to find out why.
> They said I didn't make my payment last month, in which I told them they had not mailed it, as I keep all my statements together and it was not there. She could not have cared if her hair was on fire. So now, I have last months, this months, and a late fee that costs as much as one month would have.

> She offered no resolution, and pretty much told to take a hike!
> Great way to keep customers. [6]

Still another customer complained on January 18, 2016, about the high fees, including $15 for a replacement card.

> The customer service representatives aren't very helpful, a lot of them seem to have an attitude problem, they don't have much patience & they are always in a rush to get you off the phone. There are so many fees with this card it's ridiculous. I lost my card & they charged me a $15.00 fee for a replacement. Once I pay off my balance I'm closing my account.

Another complained on January 9 about late and hidden fees and difficulties in disputing the fees with customer service.

> Be aware of this bank they charge late fees even before your bill is due date. Charge you hidden fees that you don't even tell you about it on credit your account back for the money that they charged you they also love to argue with you on the phone about your account and your statements beware.

For a consumer from Santa Ana, California, who filed a report on December 9, 2015, the problem was excessive collection calls for a small amount. As the consumer wrote:

> I closed this account due to them harassing me over the phone for a $25.00 payment. They will call you 10+ times a day at all times if you are even (1) day late.
> I requested them to not call me anymore with harassing calls and in return they closed my account. I am almost done paying these clowns off and recently tried getting a late fee waived that I was eligible for on a payment and it was waived. However they then charged me again for the same late fee AGAIN the next month, because of some clown policy they have in place. Currently filing complaint with BBB. DO NOT EVER GET A CREDIT CARD WITH THIS COMPANY.
> STAY FAR AWAY FROM MERRICK BANK! [7]

And here's another complaint from a consumer in Berkeley, California, on February 23, 2015, about excess charges and delays in getting back a deposit on a secured account after closing the account.

> Merrick Bank is a MAJOR disappointment. I was an active card member with them for over two years and recently cancelled my account. When you sign-up for a secured card to rebuild your credit, they state that they give credit limit increases regularly once you establish a good payment record. Cool I thought. It's worth it. After being a card member for over two years and paying my bill IN FULL every month without EVER BEING LATE, they raised my credit limit in this time period from my initial secured $600 to $1,100. They charge you a $36 annual fee which they bill on a monthly basis ($3 per statement) which I'm sure they do it hoping that if you don't use your card, that you will be late for the $3 so they can ding you with a late fee. To top things off, when I went to close my account to get my deposit back, the agent said it would take 60–90 days to get it back. Unbelievable. They want your money to open an account quickly and then sit on it for several weeks. Then, when you find out how horrible they are and it's time to get your deposit back, good luck.[8]

The complaints against Barclays Bank show a similar pattern of high interest fees suddenly appearing on the card, problems with reduced credit scores even though the card was initially obtained to help gain a better score and qualify for a major credit card, and poor communication and customer service in response to problems with billings or purchased items. Here is a sampling of those complaints. I have corrected some of the grammar and punctuation for easier reading.

This is from February 15, 2015, from a customer in Missouri who complained to the Better Business Bureau, which redacted certain identifying details about the customer and other companies. I have included approximations of what these dates might be.

> In brief, I unknowingly missed the promotional end date for the promotion I was under and as a result, my [$2,500] account received a [$1,300] deferred interest charge. In XX/XX/XXXX, I was accepted into a school program that required me to purchase an XXXX computer. We did not have the funds for a cash purchase, so we applied for a Barclay credit card. The Barclay card that we were offered included a XXXX deferred interest promotion on the purchase.

After buying the computer, I set up the paperless statements and Autopay, so that I wouldn't miss any payments with my busy school schedule. We planned to pay off any remaining balance on the card before the promotional period; however, I have not received any notification from Barclay regarding the ending promotional period. I thought the end date should be coming soon (around XX/XX/XXXX) so I logged onto the account on XXXX XXXX to go ahead and take care of everything and pay off the credit card. To my surprise, I found that I was XXXX weeks late and the promotional period had ended on XXXX XXXX and I had been charged [$1,300] in interest on a [$2,500] principle balance.

This interest charge was totally unexpected. I neither expected to see that the promotional period had ended nor expected such an astronomical interest charge. I called and talked to multiple managers and team managers at Barclay, and I learned what had happened. I received paperless statements, and signed up for autopay, both of which I felt were the most responsible way to handle this new credit card, but this worked against me. The e-mail notifications that come with the paperless statements do not give any indication of the approaching end date of the promotional period and no communication was received by myself, from Barclay, to inform me that the promotional period would end or that I would have a [$1,300] interest charge to my account.

I also found out that I would need to log in to the account to view the statement and see this deferred interest information; however, that was not made apparent to me in any way and I was under the impression that the autopay and e-mail notifications had negated the need for frequent account logins and statement checks. This lack of notification has caused me to be a mere XXXX weeks late and to incur a substantial interest fee.

While trying to resolve this on the phone with Barclay, I offered to pay the principal balance immediately if we could waive this interest fee, but I have not been able to achieve this. They were only willing to waive [$500] of the interest, which is helpful, but still leaves me with an [$820] interest charge. I feel like, because of the lack of communication, this interest charge snuck in on me, whilst I was attempting to do the responsible thing. I also feel like I was deceived with the meaning of "deferred interest." This was XXXX of my first credit cards, and I feel taken advantage of, because I had no idea that this is what deferred interest results in. I thought it was an analogy to 0% interest, and different companies use different terminology. I am a student in XXXX school, and my only sources of income are student loans, as my program does not allow employment. If I cannot get this resolved my only option is to pay this interest fee with another loan, maximizing my loss in this situation.

And here's another representative complaint on June 18, 2015, from a customer in California, also complaining to the Better Business Bureau.

On XXXX XXXX 2014, I cancelled my credit card with Barclays Bank. I just received a collection notice from XXXX wanting XXXX. I called Barclay Bank. They say that a bill was paid over a month after the card had been cancelled for XXXX. They never contacted me about the bill. I asked them for the phone # and address they had and it was correct. I asked them why they never contacted me. They did not know. I said I would pay the XXXX, they said they could not deal with me that I have to deal with the collection agency. The collection agency wants XXXX and will not deal. I asked if I pay the XXXX would they take it off my credit report. They said no. First I believe Barclays had no authority to pay the XXXX and should have had the store contact me. Second Barclays should have at least tried to contact me about the XXXX dollars. Now they have destroyed my credit. I am willing to pay the XXXX but they must remove it from my credit report.

In another case involving a complaint to the Better Business Bureau, from July 14, 2015, a customer found it impossible to get a fraudulent charge removed from an account belonging to the customer's elderly mother.

I am filing this on behalf of my mother who is in XXXX. Barclays Juniper had an open charge account in her name. XX/XX/XXXX they initially reported suspicious activity to me on her account via e-mail. I immediately reported it as fraudulent per their electronic website. In XX/XX/XXXX they sent a statement showing the fraudulent balance, requesting payment. This time I sent them a letter requesting they remove the charges. In XX/XX/XXXX they again sent me notice of suspicious activity. This third time I called their security number and once again reported it as fraud. I was ultimately hung up on by their agent without letting me finish what I was saying. After that I sent them a certified letter informing them to close the account immediately and that any repeated attempts to collect the disputed amounts would be referred to authorities. On XXXX XXXX they once again sent a form letter indicating the amount of [$260] is due and providing the methods that the amount can be paid. We have notified them four times and they refuse to remove the amount and keep requesting payment. We have done everything in our power to resolve this with the company but continue to be unsuccessful so we are forwarding this to you as an official complaint. Thank you for your help.

Finally, here are two more representative complaints against Barclay's on the RipOff Report. From Dan in Bristow, Virginia, posted in the RipOff Report on May 8, 2014:

Barclays Bank Delaware Barclaycard Bait & Switch Annual Fee Wilmington Nationwide. One year after signing up for a Juniper Bank MasterCard with no annual fee, I was notified that Barclays would be charging an annual fee of $99. I called customer service today and after a transfer to a "Specialist" and a transfer to "Supervisor" I was told that they would not remove the fee. I will close the account next month. [9]

From MarianneM in Los Angeles, California, posted in the RipOff Report on January 23, 2015:

Barclays Bank Damaged Credit History without a cause Nationwide. The worst customer service ever. Let the charges go $15 USD over the limit by adding the $15 interest on the day card was paid and reported to credit bureaus on the same day interest was charged. [10]

Likewise, Capital One has been subject to a litany of similar complaints.

For example, here's a plea from one very angry consumer from Menlo Park, California, at Pissed Consumer, involving a variety of charges—failure to close an account, incorrect late payment charges used to lower a credit score, and a lack of responsiveness by customer service.

PLEASE DONT BANK OR APPLY FOR CREDIT WITH CAPITAL ONE!!!! On June 20, 2015, I called Capital One to close our account. We paid our remaining balance by phone, closed our account, and cut up our card. In October, we received a call telling us our account was past due. Concerned, we called back and were informed that "due to a system error" our account remained open. Not only did our account remain open, it was now past due as the result of monthly recurring charge set up against the account. Upon calling Capital One, they were very helpful, apologized for the mistake, reversed all late fees and finance charges and also indicated that the past due would not go against our credit record.

Fast forward to January 2016, and upon running our credit to begin the mortgage qualification process we were in shock at our low credit scores. Upon reviewing the report, the low score was due primarily to the 30-day late payment posted against my record from Capital One. Confused and frustrated, I opened an investigation with Cap One, who was no longer helpful and indicate that they had no proof that our account was closed and that we were liable.

Ultimately, after 5 weeks of constant follow up, supplying phone records, sending registered letters, and filing disputes with the credit bureaus, Capital One continued to validate the late payment posting to us and to the credit bureaus. After continued calls to Capital One and the Consumer Financial Bureau we received a call from a woman at the Executive office. She listened to our story, seemed reasonable and indicated she would look into it. I faxed all the information regarding the issue again and hoped for a positive outcome. No luck. They still claimed that the account was never closed, and they had no phone records to substantiate our claim.

Having no other alternatives, I tracked down and hired a lawyer in Virginia who has jurisdiction over this case. The lawyer sent a demand letter to Capital One and the Credit Unions to remove the fraudulent late payment. I hoped that once the Legal Compliance department in Virginia received the letter we would be able to work through this issue. After several more weeks without being contacted by Capital One Legal, we received a letter from our neighbor from Capital One, which was addressed to us, but did not have the correct apartment number on the address.

Upon reviewing the letter, Capital One confirmed they reviewed the phone call request for us to close the account, but stated that "due to a system error" our account remained open. They also provided a copy of a letter dated August 11 indicating our account was not closed due to an error on their part. I was registered to receive electronic communications and never received that August 11 letter, which also was sent to the wrong address.

After calling Capital One back and explaining all the issues again, including the issue with the mailing address, under a last hope that they would see that this late payment was more their fault than ours, they still held firm and indicated we were responsible for the charges even though those charges would never have occurred without the system error that they have admitted to. You would think going through all of this effort with Capital One would have convinced them to correct the issue due to their mistake, instead, we feel we are being targeted by Capital One for a reason we don't understand. We really believe Capital One is in very corrupt company that downright lies and utilizes fraudulent practices to hide their mistakes. Please read this and never bank nor apply for credit with Capital One they are the most corrupt company I have ever dealt with. [11]

There are literally thousands of complaints about these subprime credit cards that people get to try to improve their credit. While they may work for some people, there are many problems with high interest and extra fees, as well as extra charges or cancellation of cards with the slightest delay or mix-up in making payments. And often a missed deadline on a 0 percent interest promotion means an extremely high charge because the high interest rate is calculated on the past balances. It is as if these companies set up their offers and payment arrangements so that people will not be aware of the fees and interest charges or the deadlines for a promotion ending. And then, should problems develop, the customer service people are reportedly often unresponsive and late or missed payments are immediately reported to the credit scoring companies like Experian, TransUnion, and Equifax. Thus credit scores end up going down rather than up.

So what should you do as a consumer? First, if you decide to get one of these cards, be sure to carefully read all of the fine print so that you know what the terms are. Second, be careful to note any payment dates, and if you don't get a statement, contact the company online or call to get your statement or amount due and pay it so you don't get charged for a late payment that will go on your credit record. Third, if there is a date when a promotional rate ends, be sure to get your payment in before that date so you don't get past interest charged on your card. Allow enough time for the payment to arrive before the deadline, and be aware that if a company is in the East, the cutoff will occur according to that time zone. Some have discovered their payment was late because of this time difference. Also, be prepared for the possibility of long delays if you need to reach customer service about any kind of payment, billing, or product problems.

An alternative to a subprime credit card might be to let your credit rebound naturally by simply using a debit card and monitoring your bank account closely, checking the transactions for each day online. This way, your credit score can improve naturally. You can use a debit card like a credit card for any purchases so you don't need to carry cash around. You will find that you don't really need a credit card and won't have to risk the problems that may occur with high fees and interest rates.

CANCELING PRESCREENED OR PREAPPROVED CREDIT CARD OFFERS

If you do decide you don't want to get a subprime credit card, you can stop these offers from coming. You can either opt out of receiving them for five years or permanently, as described by the FTC's Consumer Information Unit. To opt out for five years, call the toll-free number 1-888-5-OPT-OUT (1-888-567-8688) or go to www.optoutprescreen.com, operated by the major reporting companies. If you want to opt out permanently, you can start the process online at the above website and then fill out and sign the Permanent Opt-Out Election form, which you will receive after you make your initial online request.

Opting out can also help to limit a credit reporting company giving access to your credit report information, although these kinds of requests for general information are considered "soft" inquiries that don't affect your credit report. Then, too, you might want to opt out to reduce the amount of junk mail you get. However, opting out will only prevent companies from sending offers to you based on prescreening your credit information, and you may still get offers from other companies that don't use prescreening. For example, you might still get credit solicitations from other sources, such as local merchants, charities, and professional and alumni associations. To stop those mailings, as well as mail addressed to "occupant" or "resident," you have to contact each source individually.

When you do call or go to the website, be prepared to provide certain personal information, including your name, home phone number, Social Security number, and date of birth. This information is considered confidential and will only be used to process your opt-out request. If you don't have access to the Internet, you can send a written request to permanently opt out to each of the major credit reporting companies. Include the same personal information that is required online—your name, home phone number, Social Security number, and date of birth. The addresses of the major credit reporting companies, according to the FTC, are:

Experian, Opt Out, P.O. Box 919, Allen, TX 75013
TransUnion, Name Removal Option, P.O. Box 505, Woodlyn, PA
    19094
Equifax Inc., Options, P.O. Box 740123, Atlanta, GA 30374-0213
Innovis Consumer Assistance, P.O. Box 495, Pittsburgh, PA 15203

Generally, once you opt out, it may take up to sixty days before the offers stop, though the requests are processed within five days. Should you later change your mind and want to opt back in, you can always do so by calling the opt-out number or going to the opt-out website.

You can also reduce telemarketing calls about credit cards or other opportunities to increase your credit or reduce your credit card debt by contacting the federal government's National Do Not Call Registry, since telemarketers aren't supposed to call you if your number is listed. To register your phone number—or if you want more information about the registry—you can call 1-888-383-1222 or visit the Do Not Call Registry's website at www.donotcall.gov. You should get fewer marketing calls within thirty-one days after you register your number. Your number will remain there permanently until you call to remove it.

You can similarly opt out of receiving unsolicited commercial mail about credit or other sales offers from any companies that use the Direct Marketing Association's (DMA) Mail Preference Service. When you register, your name is put in a "delete" file for five years, so any direct-mail marketers or organizations using this service can see this. But you might still get mailings from other organizations that don't use this service. Additionally, you can opt out of receiving unsolicited commercial e-mail for six years from all DMA members through the DMA's Email Preference Service (eMPS). To register for these services, go to www.dmachoice.org, or you can mail your request with a $1 processing fee to the following address: DMAchoice, Direct Marketing Association, P.O. Box 643, Carmel, NY 10512.

However, before you opt out, take into consideration that these prescreened offers and other commercial e-mail can provide certain benefits, especially if you are thinking about getting a credit card. These offers can let you know what is available, enable you to compare costs between different offerings, and find the best type of credit card for your purposes. Then, too, since you have been preselected, you are likely to be accepted, barring special circumstances. Also, sometimes the terms of these offers may be better than those offered to the general public, and some credit card offerings may only be available through these prescreened offers.

Thus, these offers can be something of a mixed blessing. Some people do benefit, which is why these companies are still in business offering a legitimate product. For others, it is a kind of credit card fraud, and once you sign up for the card, the promises of the marketers become elusive and the true costs become clear.

So if you get these offers or are deciding whether to keep getting them, weigh your various options and the various benefits and downsides of getting a card. For some, the enticements of the companies may amount to fraud. Others may see these offers as a way to gain access to more credit as long as they make the payments and are fully aware of the promotional deadlines.

5

AVOIDING FREE TRIAL AND SPECIAL DISCOUNT SCAMS

Often consumers get lured into free trials and offers of special discounts because they think they are getting a good deal if they act quickly. Often these fraudsters use ads featuring celebrities, which seem to be endorsements, but they are actually defrauding the celebrities, too. Once consumers respond, they may end up with an automatic monthly charge that they have a hard time stopping. This chapter describes the warning signs to look for, how to avoid getting duped, and what to do to get these fraudulent charges reduced and to report these fraudsters to law enforcement.

HOW A FREE TRIAL AND SPECIAL DISCOUNT SCAM WORKS

The problem with the free trial or special discount offer is that it may start off as a free trial—or a product, service, or subscription you can get for a very low cost. Sometimes the only charge is for a nominal shipping fee. So it may seem like an opportunity to try something out with little to lose. But these offers may cost you real money, and you may find the product, service, or subscription is of little value. As the FTC's Consumer Information Unit advises, "Some companies use free trials to sign you up for more products—sometimes lots of products—

which can cost you lots of money as they bill you every month until you cancel."[1]

A big problem is that to take advantage of the free trial or special discount is you have to give the company your credit card information, and by clicking a button, you may find yourself agreeing to contract terms that you haven't read. After all, the contract may be hard to find, and even if you find it, it's commonly a dozen or so pages of small-print, single-spaced legal jargon. And the terms create an obligation to keep paying until you cancel—which the company makes it hard to do. Often the free trial doesn't arrive until a few days before the cancellation date, or you end up subscribing for another month because you don't realize that your free trial actually started when the company got your order and credit card information, and not when they shipped the product or you received it. By that time, you are likely to go past at least the first trial period. And then if you actually try the product—say, by opening a jar of beauty cream—you can no longer return it, so you are now responsible for paying, even though it was a "free" trial. If you try to get out of paying for it, say by closing your credit card, the nonpayment will go on your credit report, or if you delay payment while disputing it, it will be recorded as a late payment. Thus, people sometimes pay several hundred dollars just to get out of a free trial.

One possible way to stop the scammers is to go to your credit card or bank and claim fraud early on after the first unexpected charges appear on your credit card. At this point, the card company or bank will probably refund your money, and the company will not try to counter your claim (these companies often change their names and start pitching similar products), since they would rather find more victims than get caught up in fighting a fraud case. Unfortunately, many defrauded customers don't know to do this; they just resign themselves to losing the charges that appear on their credit card for the first month or two—often several hundred dollars, until their cancellation goes through.

The FTC's Consumer Information Unit advises:

> Some dishonest businesses make it tough to cancel, hiding the terms and conditions of their offers in teensy type, using pre-checked sign-up boxes as the default setting online, and putting conditions on returns and cancellations that are so strict it could be next to impossible to stop the deliveries and the billing.[2]

One of the ways the fraudsters get your credit card information for a so-called free trial is with a small shipping and handling fee, such as $4.95 or $5.95, which seems so small, you feel it's a no brainer to try out something new. So you think you're only paying a few dollars for the trial. But the company is really getting you to give out your credit card information in order to keep charging you after the trial ends, which is much sooner than you expect.

The other way these free trial offers work, as the FTC's Consumer Information Unit describes, is to enroll consumers in clubs or subscriptions, offering an introductory package of free books, CDs, magazines, or movies. The offer may sound inviting, especially if the initial offering entices you with things you might want to purchase. So you figure you are saving a lot of money. But if you sign up, you may find you have agreed to a subscription that's automatically renewed. This particular scheme isn't so nefarious as the patently fraudulent efforts to get you to sign up for a product or subscription designed to get your credit card information and trick you into paying several hundred dollars before you are able to stop it. But you could still find it difficult to stop the subscription from continuing.

A Closer Look at How a Free Trial Scam Works

Following is a closer look at one of these free trial scams—the Beau Derma and Revita Eye Scam, described previously in *Scammed* by Gini Graham Scott. One of the strategies in the company's advertising that makes the offer seem so compelling is the appearance of endorsement by major celebrities and experts, along with supporting research. Moreover, these sponsored advertorials are featured on a site that already has a built-in following, such as Facebook. So the product seems perfectly legit, and the ads convince hundreds if not thousands of victims to sign up for what seems to be a no-risk, no-obligation free trial. Using this ploy, the ad enables the fraudster to obtain victims' credit card information and put through unauthorized charges under the cover of a purported legal agreement that the victims unknowingly accept by placing a trial order for only a small shipping fee. Only later do the victims discover that they have unknowingly agreed to receive and pay for a membership and monthly automatic shipments of each product, which continue until canceled.

The payments amount to nearly $200 a month if the victim accepts the enticement to get two products together, $100 if the victim chooses only one product, although the ad convinces most to get the complementary products together for even more benefits. As a result, hundreds if not thousands of victims have lost hundreds of dollars, as described on consumer complaint sites, such as RipOffReport (www.ripoffreport.com) or the Better Business Bureau. For some, the loss had devastating consequences, since they were unemployed or living on very little income. Undoubtedly there are many more victims who did not post their complaints, since only a small percentage of victims report their victimization.

Had a prospective customer decided to check out the validity of the offer, it would have been clear that the company was a scam. For instance, they would have seen that the Better Business Bureau in Santa Ana, California, where the companies were based (though it seems they move around and have a similar scam with two other beauty products), gave both companies an F rating, due to 26 complaints filed against Beau Derma and 19 complaints against Revita Eye. They would have seen dozens of complaints against these companies on Scamorg.com, and 215 complaints against Beau Derma and 31 complaints against Revita Eye on Ripoffreport.com.

The complaints are typically made jointly against both companies, since they share the same address, follow almost exactly the same procedures, and have the same terms of service contracts, though they have different numbers for customer service. Given the large number of complaints charging credit card fraud, and some additionally reporting damages from the products, it is surprising that the owners of these companies are not in jail, or at least under investigation. But one difficulty in pursuing criminal or legal actions against these companies is that after a few months they move to another state, have another company name, and have new products they use for their come on. Often such companies are in foreign countries. Plus the individual losses are below felony limits, such as $950 or more in California, so with multiple victims in different states legal action is more difficult.

In any event, the basic scam involves advertising an antiaging product, Beau Derma, which is supposed to produce a smoother, younger-looking skin, and a recommended companion product, Revita Eye, which supposedly removes wrinkles around the eyes. These products are advertised as being used, endorsed, and highly praised by well-known celebrities. Photos show these celebrities or others before and after using the product, although these might easily be pictures that were taken at different times for another purpose. While different free trial scams are directed toward different target markets, in this case, the primary market for these antiaging products is largely women thirty and older, and the implication from these before-and-after photos is that by using the product, women will look much younger after using the product. One of the expert endorsers is supposedly Dr. Oz, who allegedly recommended the products on his show.

To illustrate the seductive power of these ads, one of the company's ads on a Yahoo news feed featured some before-and-after photos of a woman who used the product. The ad copy highlighted the great benefits of the product, suggested that well-known celebrities used it, and claimed it was endorsed by major health and medical professionals, most notably Dr. Oz.

The company also offered a "free" fourteen-day trial, which made trying this product sound like a "no-lose" proposition. The only cost was supposedly for the shipping—$4.95 for one product, $5.95 for the other—and the sign-up form recommended that one order both products, since they worked effectively together. Supposedly, a customer could cancel at the end of the trial period if he or she didn't like the product, with no further obligation. So, on its face, this offer seemed like an attractive one, and it sounded like at most one would be out about $10 for shipping if one didn't like the product.

To start the trial, the victim would fill in the requested information, which seemed quite standard—name, delivery address, city, state, zip, e-mail, phone number, and credit card information. Then, to finalize the order, the victim would click a button indicating that he or she accepted the terms of the sale—again a common practice by many companies online. Commonly victims simply click automatically, without realizing that this constitutes a contract, since clicking an acceptance button is a routine part of online sales. In this case, the victim would probably not see any link for reading the terms of agreement, which was buried at the bottom of the company website. And it was unlikely that anyone would read it, anyway, since it was a ten-page, single-spaced document.

About a week later, the victim would receive two packages as USPS tracked shipments, which meant that the victim would later learn that the free trial had only about six or seven more days to go, because the trial period was counted from the day the order was placed, not from when it arrived. If the victim was busy with other things and didn't open the package for several days, he or she might only have one or two more days of the free trial left to go—and in some cases, the trial period might have already expired.

This scam, like many of its kind, also offered a substandard product—or a product that could have been bought directly at a substantially lower price. For example, the Beau Derma product came in a small white jar with only the words "Beau Derma" on the side, while the Revita Eye product came in a thin lavender bottle with ultra-tiny lettering on it, so it was unreadable to the naked eye. There were no instructions in either package as to how the product should be used, though one would normally expect such information with a medical or health product, such as guidelines on how much should be applied, where, how often, what results to expect, and any warnings about potential side effects.

If the victim didn't act quickly enough to cancel the free trial without actually using the product so it could be returned—at the victim's cost—two payments—one for $85.95 for Revita Eye and the other for $89.95 for Beau Derma—would be charged to his or her credit or debit card, exactly fourteen days after the shipping charges for the products were posted.

What if a victim immediately called the companies to complain that he or she had never authorized this charge? For one thing, making it even more difficult to complain, there were two different companies and two different customer service people to respond to, even though the victim had originally placed a single order. But the order was for two separate products, and the time required to talk to a customer service person was doubled. Moreover, the customer service people seemed to be trained to deflect any complaints and avoid giving any refunds by reminding people that the trial period had ended and they had agreed to a contract, so they had an obligation to pay regardless of what they thought of the product or even if they hadn't yet had a chance to try it.

For instance, in a typical call, one victim had an extended debate with the customer service rep, who claimed she owed the money because she had received a thirty-day supply of both products and didn't cancel her subscription before the end of the trial period. So she owed the money for the product that was already sent to her, and if the subscription wasn't canceled, she would get another shipment for the same amount in thirty days.

Moreover, though the victim said she wanted to return the product, the customer rep said she couldn't because it was after the fourteen-day trial period, so her card was already charged. She could only return the product with a return merchandise authorization number or RMA. But because it was after the trial period, the customer rep couldn't give her that number.

Even if a customer expressed dissatisfaction with the product, the customer service rep was trained to sell more. For instance, she told the victim, "If you want to keep the product, I'm authorized to give you a 15 percent discount," and when the victim said that was unacceptable, she increased the discount to 33 percent and finally to 50 percent, and since the victim had already been charged for the product, she could refund the difference on her credit card. In other words, not only had the victim been scammed, but the customer service reps were trained to see if they could get even more for a substandard or overpriced product.

But even if the victim said the 50 percent discount still wasn't acceptable and that she wanted to return the product, which she hadn't even tried, the customer service rep resumed claiming that she couldn't return it because it was after the trial period. Even if the victim now spoke of filing a complaint with her bank and credit card company to reverse the charge, the rep had a ready answer for that: "You can't do that because the company will win, because you signed an iron-clad agreement with them."

At this point, the victim might be likely to respond, "What agreement," whereupon the rep would explain. "There's a Terms of Service Agreement on the company's website." But what if the customer didn't see this agreement buried in small type on the bottom of the company website? Again, the rep would throw back the responsibility on the customer, saying, "It's your responsibility to read this agreement, and since you didn't, you are bound by those rules." If the customer argued that these terms weren't made clear in the advertisement, the customer service rep would fall back to offering a 50 percent discount to keep the product, since "You are a good customer," as if she had a script to follow in response to various customer complaints.

At this point, most victims would give up in the face of repeated claims that they had agreed to a binding agreement and didn't return the product in time. But one victim found that after she repeated that she would complain to her credit card company and her bank, after about a half hour of arguing back and forth, the rep relented and said she would issue an RMA, but the customer would have to return the product within fourteen days for it to be effective. The victim assured her that she would return it the next day, and later she did get an e-mail confirming the return authorization. This illustrates that a very determined victim might be able to get a company rep to issue a refund—although the simpler way to deal with this is to go directly to your credit card company or bank and charge fraud. But this company makes the return and refund process more difficult, since the victim still has a second product return to negotiate with another customer service rep at a different phone number, even though the products were shipped from the same Santa Ana address.

No wonder there were so many complaints about this particular scam—over two hundred complaints about Beau Derma and over fifty for Revita Eye on RipOffReport.com. There were also several dozen listings on Scamorg.com. Other complaints were on Yahoo and Yelp. And the Better Business Bureau in Santa Ana rated both companies an F because of the large number of complaints—twenty-six for Beau Derma, nineteen for Revita Eye.

The gist of these complaints was much the same—consumers suddenly found two purchases for nearly $90 each charged to their card, and when they called to complain, the customer service rep gave them multiple offers of discounts to keep the product or told them they weren't allowed to return it because the trial period was over. In some cases, the victims had two or three charges on their card before they were able to cancel their orders and stop the charges. In many cases, people gave up trying to get a refund and complained of losing $200 to $550 to the company. And many who did try the product reported that it had made their skin and eyes even worse by causing burning, peeling, and flaking, so they felt doubly victimized.

Though this victim not only got the rep to issue a full refund from her bank of the $89.95 and $85.95 for the two products after filing an affidavit that the charges were unauthorized, the vast majority of victims who complained about their experience weren't so fortunate; they felt helpless and lost their money.

The Free Trial Agreement

As for the agreement, which all customers have to accept by clicking a button to participate in the free trial, it was not only difficult to find on the company website in small type at the very bottom of the home page, but it was also unlikely that any potential customer would read this agreement. Nor would they even understand that this agreement, which might be unenforceable, made it clear that this was not really a free trial. Among other things, the agreement stated the following:

> By using, visiting, or browsing the Website, as well as placing an order with Beau Derma (or RevitaEye) through the Website, You accept, without limitation or qualification, these Terms of Use and agree, without limitation, to the terms of Our Privacy Statement. If You do not agree to be bound by these Terms of Use and Privacy Statement, You should exit the Website immediately. By accessing, using or ordering products through the Website, You affirm that You have read this Agreement and understand, agree, and consent to all Terms contained herein.

But what if someone doesn't see this agreement or read it? How can they be bound by these terms—and what legitimate sales company would expect a customer seeking a free trial of a product to read a ten-page single-spaced document? The agreement goes on to bind the person to its terms anyway:

> You manifest Your agreement to the Terms in this document by any act demonstrating Your assent thereto, including clicking any button containing the words "I Agree"; "Rush My Order"; "Submit" or similar syntax, or by merely accessing the Website, whether You have read these terms or not.

It continues with a product disclaimer, which contradicts the claims made in the ads and on the website, since the implication in the ad copy and photos is that the product will improve a person's skin as an anti-aging product. The disclaimer seems to be designed to relieve the company of any responsibility for any problems caused by the product's use or by the company's failure to include any instructions for proper use with either product. As the disclaimer states:

> I understand the statements regarding these products have not been evaluated by the Food and Drug Administration. This product is not intended to diagnose, treat, cure or prevent any disease. . . . I understand the information on this Website or in emails is designed for educational purposes only and is not intended to be a substitute for informed medical advice or care. I understand I should not use this information to diagnose or treat any health problems or illnesses without consulting my doctor. I also understand that Beau Derma is not intended to be used to treat any type of medical condition.

But in contradiction to this, the advertisement for the product does promote this product as providing skin care and revitalization.

The refund policy also contradicts this being a free trial, since, among other things, the agreement states that the company will only "credit one returned unopened product per customer if the received package is postmarked within 30 days of the original order date and included with a RMA number obtained from customer service." But if this is a free trial, you have to open the package to try the product, which makes it impossible to return. And the customer service people seem to be trained to deny an RMA in any case.

Moreover, the contract makes it difficult to keep the trial from turning into a recurring monthly subscription, with monthly charges of $89.95 for Beau Derma and $85.95 for Revita Eye. It is not clear until you get hit with these charges that the fourteen-day trial membership begins on the day of the application, not when you actually get the product. As the agreement states:

> You agree that if you do not send us notice of cancellation of your trial membership from the expiration of your trial membership terms, we shall automatically and without further notice: convert your trial membership to a standard RECURRING MONTHLY SUBSCRIPTION to Beau Derma Services, at the standard one

month membership rate; renew your monthly membership to the Beau Derma Services for successive periods of one month each at the then current standard one-month membership rate, which on our auto-shipment program will have a new 30-day supply sent to you every month. . . .

TO CANCEL AUTOMATIC RENEWAL AT THE END OF THE PAID TRIAL MEMBERSHIP PERIOD, YOU MUST NOTI-FY Beau Derma PRIOR TO THE END OF THE PAID TRIAL PERIOD, BY CONTACTING Beau Derma BY TELEPHONE.

But since people who place orders are unlikely to realize that the fourteen-day trial period begins when they place their order, not when they get their product, they are unlikely to discover they have a charge for these products on their credit card account or bank statement until *after* the fourteen days have passed.

The contract then goes on, authorizing Beau Derma to charge the customer's credit card using the information entered on the sign-up page until and unless it is notified of a cancellation. In fact, there is even a clause that states that anyone that fraudulently reports a lost or stolen credit card to obtain goods or services from the site or fraudulently reports an unauthorized charge on their credit card is liable to Beau Derma for "liquidated damages of $25,000." Further, this liquidated damages liability doesn't limit "any other liability you may have for breaches(es) of any other terms, conditions, promises and warranties set forth in this Agreement."

Should someone actually read the agreement and want to protest the unexpected, unauthorized charges, this statement that one could incur a huge liability by simply claiming the charge was unauthorized might scare one away from making such a claim. Or it could give the company the basis for fraudulently seeking even more money from someone in court or as a settlement to avoid fighting a case in court.

Still other terms provide for the complete indemnity of "Beau Derma, its affiliates, officers, directors, shareholders, employees, independent contractors, telecommunications providers, and agents from any and all claims, actions, loss, liabilities, expense, costs, or demands, including, but not limited to, reasonable legal and accounting fees, which are not limited to Florida's Statewide Uniform Guidelines for Taxation of Costs in Civil Actions, for all damages directly, indirectly, and/or consequently resulting or allegedly resulting from Your use, misuse, or inability to use the Website, or Your breach of any of these terms and conditions of this agreement."

It was not clear at the time why Florida's law should apply, since the company was then based in Santa Ana, California. But there were several similar free trial promotions for antiaging products from companies based in South Beach, Hollywood, Boca Raton, and Miami Beach, Florida, so perhaps the real base of this company was there. But wherever the Beau Derma and the Revita Eye company (or companies) were actually located, it would seem that this provision is intended to protect the company and its owners from any claims of it being a scam. Moreover, there are even provisions that individuals agree not to "pursue arbitration on a consolidated or classwide basis," presumably to protect the company from the many individuals who have been scammed joining together in a class action against it.

Moreover, the company claims that it can change any provisions in this agreement at any time and that customers agree to review these terms and conditions each time they visit the website, because, "Your continued use of the Website following the posting of any changes to these terms and conditions constitutes Your acceptance of such changes." Moreover, in this agreement, Beau Derma (and Revita Eye in virtually the same agreement) states that it has no obligation to provide users with a notice of any change to this document.

In short, this is a contract that seems to be designed to enable the company to protect itself legally from complaints that it is scamming consumers. The vast number of complaints by people who have lost money suggests that most people are taken in by the scam and are unable to get back their money, in many cases because they give up. Most of those filing complaints lost as much as $500 to $600 when their card was repeatedly charged.

It is also significant that there is nothing up front about the cost of a subscription to get these products each month after the free trial period. That information only comes after the charges appear on the credit card unless the customer actually reads the Terms of Agreement. Rather, victims simply discover they are supposedly bound by a contract they have not seen or read in advance. In fact, the contract specifically states the individual is bound just by clicking a button on the website, regardless of whether he or she has read the agreement. Clicking the button supposedly provides that acceptance.

It seems questionable that this could be a legal contract. How can one be bound by a contract one hasn't read when clicking the button doesn't provide the person with a clear explanation of what this offer of a free trial really means? Rather, the contract would seem to be designed to support a scam to charge victims almost $180 a month for two products that come with no instructions for use and in some cases damage the skin rather than improve a person's appearance as advertised.

THE MAJOR ELEMENTS OF A SCAM

The Beau Derma/Revita Eye scam is a powerful one that includes the major elements of typical scams that continue to entrap victims. The scammers also benefit from using a number of product and company names and locations, so once one scam generates enough negative blow-back, the scammers can easily change the names of the products and the company to continue essentially the same scam under another guise, such as promoting other antiaging products called Revitol and Dermology, as one victim, GLS from Kent, Washington (January 16, 2015) observed:

> I purchased the trial of BeauDerma and RevitaEye before reading consumer reviews. After reading multiple reviews and your site I became concerned. Investigating, I found that different products; Revitol and Dermology are presented in the same manner. All the products have identical advertising; text, same before-after pictures and the same testimonials. They also have "Dr. Oz recommended" and the same "Trial" offer. This appears to be deceptive advertising.
>
> Since I read of the unexpected charges many people incurred, I'm cancelling my order immediately via my credit card company. It looked too good to be true and it was!

The major elements of these kinds of scams are the following:

1. An initial enticing offer, which can take the form of a compelling powerful ad, to be discussed further in the next section.

2. A claim that the prospect will have a limited or no obligation, such as by offering a seemingly "no-risk" or "no-obligation" free trial, which really isn't free.

3. The concealing of specific information about the agreement that might show what the prospect is agreeing to, such as Beau Derma's and Revita Eye's ten-page, single-spaced contract, which claims that the customer is opting for a membership with recurring automated charged and not just a free trial.

4. An easy way to sign up, such as a seemingly innocuous "click" button.

5. Effective advertising with expert and celebrity endorsements and purported scientific research support.

6. A requirement to provide credit card information, which the company can check by charging a small amount for an initial shipping and handling fee.

7. Barriers to getting a refund, which include: (a) a time-limit for canceling the initial free trial that is unlikely for victims to meet, given the time required to receive the product; (b) difficulty in canceling orders or getting a refund due to poor customer service; (c) the hassle of seeking a refund through one's credit card company or bank and possibly having to set up another credit card to avoid future unauthorized charges.

8. A product or service of low quality or even have negative effects.

Unfortunately, it is difficult to stop these kinds of scams, like many of the other scams described in this book, since the amount scammed is relatively low for each individual and it is very time consuming to pursue an individual case, especially since the scammers move around or may have an operation in multiple jurisdictions, states, and even countries. So generally, the best you can do is to beware of the warning signs so you don't get scammed, and if you do, you can report the scam for insurance purposes. But otherwise, it is unlikely that law enforcement will get involved.

THE POWER OF ADVERTISING TO LURE VICTIMS

The secret to the success of scams like the Beau Derma and Revita offers is in the ads. The ads convince individuals to click on an innocuous-looking free trial offer, asking them for name, address, phone, and e-mail. If a person tries to leave the page, there is often a dialogue box asking "do you really want to leave this page?" If a person puts in contact information, he or she is directed to another page to enter credit card information for the small shipping fee and to click on a box indicating an agreement to the company's terms and conditions. So lulled by the convincing nature of the ad, the individual clicks an acceptance, and so begins the scam.

What is so persuasive about the ad? First, a typical ad begins with a series of claims that a well-known celebrity has used the product successfully, that a widely known doctor has testified to the great power of the product, and that this endorsement has been featured in well-known publications and news services. In particular, one of these ads begins with the comment: "You won't believe the secret wrinkle mix that Jane Fonda's been using to destroy her wrinkles in seconds. Women everywhere are using it now!"—Dr. Oz. Then, the names of six well-known media brands are featured below the headline: *Yahoo!*, *Woman's Day*, *Vanity Fair*, *Time*, *People*, and *AOL*. Then, there is a photo of Jane Fonda, with the image of the Beau Derma product in the background, along with the caption: "Can you believe Jane Fonda is almost 80 years old and without Botox or surgery!"

Ads may then point out other celebrities who use the product followed by before-and-after photos. Following this buildup, ads may briefly present some scientific basis for the products working and state that it is one of the only products—if not the only product—you can buy that works according to this scientific evidence. If the customer still needs convincing, the ad may also claim that the company put the products to a test with various subjects, highlighting particular subjects who supposedly had great results.

Next, the ad invites readers to try the product for themselves with a free trial, often a special offer that is supposedly ending in a few days or has limited quantities, and concludes with comments from a dozen people on social media, who state they were very happy using the product.

In sum, such ads present a compelling case, featuring celebrity endorsements, a scientific explanation of why the product works so well, before-and-after pictures of people who used it in a test, an invitation to respond quickly and not miss out on the special offer, and testimonials from happy users.

Given all of this convincing buildup, why would prospects think to question the validity of the offer? After all, everything about the ad seems so legitimate and convincing. Thus, given their proven success, scammers use such ads for different products from different companies again and again. In effect, they are like the wolf in *Little Red Riding Hood* using his wiles to lure Little Red into a trap from which she needed help in order to escape. While in the traditional story, a huntsman saves the day, in this case, apart from a bank or credit card company reversing the charges, there has been little recourse because law enforcement has done little to help the victims.

THE LACK OF ATTENTION BY LAW ENFORCEMENT

Given the extensive number of victims of these scammers, why hasn't law enforcement done anything to stop them? Many victims have even noted that they alerted their local law enforcement, district attorney, or attorney general. But so far there seems to have been little or no response. Why? There appear to be a number of reasons.

- Law enforcement is overwhelmed by the vast number of Internet consumer fraud cases.
- Consumer fraud cases can be very time consuming and difficult to prosecute, given the large number of victims in multiple cities and states, involving multiple jurisdictions.
- A relatively small amount of money is lost by each individual victim, meaning that for each victim, the fraud would be considered a misdemeanor. A loss of $950 or more is required in many jurisdictions to turn a monetary loss into a felony grand theft. Combined, the losses from the scam may be in the millions, but individually the losses are small.
- The company can claim a legal cover in its "Terms and Conditions Agreement" document, asserting that the victims agreed by click-

ing an acceptance button, even if the victims didn't find or read this document. This legal cover would presumably turn any claim of an unauthorized purchase into a contract matter, making it a civil case, although this cover might be undermined by looking at the many victims making the same claims and the combined losses suffered by all of them.

- Only a small number of victims have reported their cases to law enforcement, even though hundreds have complained on consumer complaint websites.
- On the surface, the ads look very legitimate. The scam comes when customers place their orders and get products that may not be the real products and find themselves signed up for a membership with automatic payments. Customer service reps make it seem like a legitimate business by claiming that the victim must follow the terms of the agreement. Thus, for law enforcement, it might seem complicated and time consuming to prove this relatively small transaction for any single victim is actually illegal.
- The perpetrators appear to be very elusive. The business address they use may be a temporary one or just a mailing address, and they may move around from city to city or country to country. Moreover, it would appear that the same perpetrators are behind similar scams using different names and addresses, so they could easily stop promoting one scam to elude a law enforcement crackdown and promote something else with a different name and location.
- Without fully knowing the extent of a scam based on the number of victims and the total money lost, law enforcement may give it less priority than other scams or other crimes generally.

In sum, despite the proliferation of these scams, it would seem there could be many reasons why they might not be subject to a crackdown by law enforcement.

HOW TO PROTECT YOURSELF FROM A FREE TRIAL OR SPECIAL DISCOUNT SCAM

What should you do to protect yourself from falling into the free trial or special discount trap? And what should you do if you have been a victim? Here are some general guidelines.

- *Distinguish between a genuine offer of a free trial or special discount and a scam.* Not every free trial or special discount is a scam. Some legitimate retail stores and companies do offer introductory programs to get new clients or increase sales. A new professional in town may make such offers to get some testimonials to help build his or her business. The ones to watch out for are the so-called free offers that are mostly perpetrated online, by unsolicited phone calls, or through the mail, where you have to turn over your credit card information. Don't get caught up by the claimed testimonials, celebrity endorsements, and research evidence, since this can all be faked.
- *Check out the company before you sign.* One way to do this is to go to the various consumer complaint sites to see if the company is listed, as well as check with the Better Business Bureau (www. bbb.org).
- *Recognize that a free trial offer can be presented as an upsell when you go to buy another product in response to an ad on the Internet or other media.* For instance, when you call to buy a product, you may be offered a trial membership in a club or some other service. If you have to give your credit card number, know that you will have charges added to your card if you don't cancel by a certain date.
- *Check your credit card or bank statement regularly.* If unexpected charges are posted to your account, you will be in a better position to respond immediately.
- *Immediately call the company's customer service line to cancel the service and reverse any charges.* If you encounter any resistance or have trouble reaching a customer service rep, file a complaint. It is important to call both to give the company the benefit of the doubt and to provide you with evidence you can report to your

credit card company or bank that the company charged your card without authorization and would not refund your money.

- *Once you feel certain you have been scammed and the company won't do anything to refund your money, call your credit card company or bank.* Normally, they will start a dispute resolution process and give you the benefit of the doubt. You will have to explain why you believe you were the victim of a scam, and they will contact the company for an explanation. Often the company won't respond, or if it does, the card company will give you an opportunity to respond back. When you do, the credit card company will likely give you the benefit of the doubt and refund your money. In the event your credit card company has gotten numerous complaints about this company, it may cancel the company's ability to put through charges.[3] If you have a debit card that you are using as a credit card, such as a debit card through Master-Card or Visa, you can contact either the credit card company or your bank, but don't do both, since that is a duplicative effort. Generally, it will be faster if you go to your bank and file a claim of fraud affidavit. You will normally get the money back by the next business day, whereas with a credit card company, you have to wait several days or a week or two, while the company investigates.
- *Change your credit card.* This way, the fraudster can't put through any more charges on your card. Be sure to notify any companies that are putting through approved regular payments so they will have your new number.
- *File complaints about your experience.* Various consumer protection agencies and websites are active to help protect consumers from experiencing what happened to you. One agency to contact is your state Consumer Protection Agency (go to https://www.usa.gov/state-consumer). You can also file a complaint with the Better Business Bureau at its website (www.bbb.org). There are also various consumer scam reporting sites, as mentioned earlier, such as RipOff Report (http://www.ripoffreport.com), Scambusters (http://www.scambusters.org), and ConsumerAffairs (https://www.consumeraffairs.com/review).

6

CREDIT CARD AND SERVICE SCAMS

Aside from the many credit card scams that charge your card, there are many scams that target people who need credit or need help recovering money after they have paid for products with their cards but have never received those products. Here is a sampling of these different types of scams that have been identified by the FTC's Consumer Information Unit.

CREDIT REPAIR SCAMS

There are some legitimate credit repair companies that can help you increase your credit score. Mostly they recommend that you get a subprime credit card or write letters to dispute past claims for missed or delayed payments that are still on your card. This strategy often works because the creditor doesn't respond, so the claim is removed, although these are things you could do yourself. Many companies, however, take advantage of those with poor credit by charging a fee and then not doing much to help you. Some may actually engage in illegal activities, such as guiding you to submit false information.

What You Can Do for Yourself

It's important to realize that no quick fix works. You can improve your credit report legitimately, but as the FTC notes, it "takes time, a conscious effort, and sticking to a personal debt repayment plan." Thus, despite the credit repair companies' claims of quickly removing all kinds of black marks on your credit report, such as bankruptcies, judgments, liens, and bad loans, or helping you create a new credit identity, those efforts often don't work or are illegal. As the FTC points out: "no one can legally remove accurate and timely negative information from a credit report."[1]

What you can do, at no charge to you, is ask for an investigation to learn what information is in your file so you can dispute it as inaccurate or incomplete. If it's accurate, it's there for good, though sometimes when you write a letter questioning the accuracy, the company won't bother to respond and then the information will get removed on a technicality. Certainly, you can hire a company to investigate for you and send in the letters, which some people do. But whatever a credit repair company can do for you legally, you can do for yourself at little or no cost.

Knowing Your Rights

You don't need to pay a credit repair company to find out about your credit status or dispute errors, outdated items, or anything incorrectly on your credit report due to fraud. Here are your rights according to the FTC:

- You can get a free credit report if any company takes an adverse action against you, such as denying your application for credit, insurance, or employment. However, you have to ask for your report within sixty days of being notified of the company's action against you. You will then get the name, address, and phone number of the consumer reporting company that has provided the information used to deny you credit.
- You are also entitled to one free report a year under a number of conditions: if your report is inaccurate because of fraud including identity theft; if you are unemployed and plan to look for a job within sixty days; or if you are on welfare.
- You are also able to get a free copy of your credit report each year if you only ask for it from each of the nationwide credit reporting companies—Equifax, Experian, and TransUnion. You can get all

these reports at the same time, or you can make your requests at any time within the year, such as getting a report from one of the companies every four month. To get a copy of your report, visit www.annualcreditreport.com or call 1-877-322-8228.

- If there are any mistakes or outdated items on your credit report, you can contact both the credit reporting company and the company, person, or organization providing this information about you to the credit reporting company. There is no charge to dispute these mistakes or outdated items, and the reporting company and information provider are required to correct any incorrect or incomplete information.

Getting Additional Information about Your Credit Score

Besides getting a free report from these companies once a year, you can also get regular information about the status of your credit score by subscribing to reports from the individual credit reporting services. These updates can also let you know if you have been the victim of a fraud, such as someone using your card to make purchases.

You can subscribe to Experian (http://www.experian.com) for about $18 a month, although you may be able to get their special discounted subscription for about $9 a month. You can create an account with Credit Karma (www.creditkarma.com), which can provide your current score with TransUnion or Equifax at no charge. This report on your score and other credit information, such as the number of inquiries on your account, is updated every seven days. A reason there is no charge is that Credit Karma has arrangements with various credit services that offer credit cards and show the likelihood, called "Approval Odds," of your getting them based on your current credit scores, although there is no guarantee that you will be able to secure a particular offer. You can also separately subscribe to TransUnion or Equifax, and Experian offers a package price for subscribing to all three services—about $34 a month.

While these services take into account the all-important FICO score, which is used to see if you qualify for various loans and services, they generally have slightly different scores because they take into consideration different factors and weigh them differently. Also, some information providers submit information to one credit reporting company but not others. For instance, one woman had a 610 score with Experian, a 697 score with TransUnion, and a 707 score with Equifax; and when she applied for a secured credit card with her bank, the bank officer advised her that her score was 640. At least you can get a general idea of your approximate credit worth, but allow for some variation from the different companies.

How to Dispute Inaccurate Information Due to Fraud or Other Reasons

According to the FTC, you should write to the credit reporting company and indicate what information is inaccurate or fraudulently included in your credit report. You can use the following sample letter provided by the FTC to guide you in writing your letter.

[Your Name]
[Your Address]
[Your City, State, Zip Code]

[Date]

Complaint Department
[Company Name]
[Street Address]
[City, State, Zip Code]

Dear Sir or Madam:

I am writing to dispute the following information in my file. I have circled the items I dispute on the attached copy of the report I received.

This item [identify item(s) disputed by name of source, such as creditors or tax court, and identify type of item, such as credit account, judgment, etc.] is [inaccurate or incomplete] because [describe what is inaccurate or incomplete and why]. I am requesting that the item be removed [or request another specific change] to correct the information.

Enclosed are copies of [use this sentence if applicable and describe any enclosed documentation, such as payment records and court documents] supporting my position. Please reinvestigate this [these] matter[s] and [delete or correct] the disputed item[s] as soon as possible.

Sincerely,
Your name

Enclosures: [List what you are enclosing.]

You should include copies, not any originals, of any documents that support your claim, which could include a police report if you have reported the scam to the police. Besides including your complete name and address, you should clearly indicate in your letter each item in your report that you dispute. State the facts about what happened and the reasons you dispute this information, and ask that it be removed or corrected. To further indicate what you are disputing, enclose a copy of your report and circle or check the items you are questioning. Then, send your letter by certified mail, "return receipt requested," so you can show that the credit reporting company got your letter. Keep a copy of your dispute letter and enclosures for your records. Perhaps keep a file for your fraud or other claims of inaccuracies in your report.

Once you file your claim, credit report companies must investigate the question items within thirty days—the one exception is if they consider a dispute frivolous. But presumably your fraud claim is not, so they have to forward all of the relevant data you have provided about the fraud or inaccuracy to the organization that provided the information. Once this information provider gets this notice of dispute, it has to investigate, review the relevant information, and report the results of its investigation to the credit reporting company. Then, should the investigation show the disputed information is inaccurate due to fraud or other reason, the information provider has to notify the nationwide credit reporting company so it can correct your file.

After that, the credit reporting company has to give you the results of any investigation in writing, as well as a free copy of your report if the dispute results in a change—and after that it cannot put that disputed information back in your file unless the information provider verifies that it is accurate and complete. The credit reporting company also has to send you a written notice with the name, address, and phone number of the information provider, and if you request it, the company has to send notices of this correction to anyone who got a copy of your report in the past six months and anyone who got a copy of your report for employment purposes in the past two years.

If the investigation doesn't resolve the dispute, you can ask the credit reporting company to put a statement of the dispute in your file and in future reports. You can also ask the credit reporting company to give your statement to anyone who recently got a copy of your report, though you may need to pay for this service.

Besides notifying the credit reporting company, you should also tell the creditor or other information provider, in writing, that you have disputed an item, and include copies of documents supporting your position. After that, if the provider reports the item to a consumer reporting company, it has to include a notice of your dispute, and if the information is deemed inaccurate, the provider cannot report this again.

While these steps can certainly be used for all types of disputes, they are especially useful in a case where you are a fraud victim, since that could very likely lead to inaccurate information being placed in your report, and you want to report this problem as soon as possible to clean up anything negative on your report related to that fraud. Once that misinformation is removed, your score should go up.

Knowing What Can and Can't Go Away

Sometimes credit repair companies will make certain claims that they can't actually deliver on. For example, according to the FTC, they will say things like: "We can remove bankruptcies, judgments, liens, and bad loans from your credit file forever!" "We can erase your bad credit—percent guaranteed," or "Create a new credit identity—legally."

But in fact, these companies can't erase negative information that is accurate before the time limit for including that information is up. If someone promises to resolve everything with a new identity for you, that's illegal and can result in fines or prison time. More specifically, here are the lengths of time these negative listings will remain on your report:

- A credit reporting company can report most accurate negative information for seven years.
- Information on a bankruptcy can be reported for ten years.
- Information about an unpaid judgment against you can be reported for seven years or until the statute of limitations runs out, whichever is longer—though if the unpaid judgment is discharged in a bankruptcy, that has to be reported.

The seven- or ten-year reporting period starts from the date the event occurred. However, there is no time limit under certain conditions: if the report is about a criminal conviction; if you are applying for a job paying more than $75,000 a year; and if you apply for more than $150,000 worth of credit or life insurance.

Should a credit repair company claim it can beat these deadlines and remove accurate information sooner than that, it is lying. As they say, time heals all wounds, and likewise, you need the required time to remove the negative items on your credit report. A credit repair company can't do this—and if it tries, well, as they also say, time wounds all heels!

Avoiding Credit Repair Scams

Now that you are aware of the basic laws and steps you can take to repair your own credit, you are better able to assess what a credit repair company can legitimately do for you—mostly by saving you time in carrying out the steps to correct inaccurate information, and you are better able to know when you are being wooed by a credit repair scammer. According to the FTC, the signs of a scammer include the following:

- Requires payment up front before they do any work for you
- Tells you not to directly contact the credit reporting companies
- Tells you to dispute information on your credit report, even if it's accurate, usually on the theory that if you indicate a dispute, the other company won't respond, so you'll win by default—which is true, but you could do it yourself instead of paying the company to doing this

- Tells you to give false information on your applications for credit or a loan, again, on the theory that the company you have applied to won't check, but once they do, they will generally uncover the lie
- Doesn't explain your legal rights, when they explain what they can do for you

A credit repair company is scamming you because they are not following the requirements of the Credit Repair Organization Act (CROA), which was passed to cut down on fraudulent credit repair operations. The essence of this act is that it is illegal for a credit repair company to lie to you about what they can do for you or to charge you before they perform their services. More specifically, according to the FTC, which enforces this law, a credit repair company has to explain the following:

- Your legal rights in a written contract that details the services they will perform
- Your three-day right to cancel without any charge
- How long it will take to get results, which means the length of time before you start to see an increase in your credit score along with any incorrect or fraudulent information on your report
- The total cost you will pay for the service, which is typically around $1,000–$1,500
- Any guarantees of what the company will do—and what it legally can do

WHY YOU CAN'T GET A NEW CREDIT IDENTITY

One of the claims a credit repair scammer will make is that the company can provide you with a "new credit identity" that will enable you to hide a bad credit history or a bankruptcy. You just have to pay them, and then they will provide you with a nine-digit number that looks like a Social Security number although they may call it a CPN for a "credit profile number" or a "credit privacy number." Or they may tell you to apply for an Employer Identification Number—an EIN—from the IRS. Such a number is a legitimate number, generally provided to non-profit organizations, which use that number to report financial information to the IRS and Social Security Administration. But an EIN can't substitute for your Social Security number, nor can a CPN. Or sometimes the company may sell you a Social Security number taken from a child.

In any case, once you get this number, a credit card scammer may tell you to apply for credit using this number rather than your own Social Security number. They may even tell you this process is legal, but the FTC considers it a scam. In fact, if you use a stolen Social Security number as your own, you are involved in identity theft and fraud yourself.

Accordingly, if you do follow the advice of a credit repair scammer and commit fraud yourself, you may find you are in legal trouble, because you can be accused of a federal crime. As the FTC notes, it is a federal crime to "lie on a credit or loan application . . . misrepresent your Social Security number . . . (or) obtain an EIN from the IRS under false pretenses."[2]

In short, if a credit repair company invites you to engage in any of these activities, it is a sign this is a credit repair scammer. You could end up paying fines or going to prison for committing a federal crime if you take their advice.

Reporting Fraud by a Credit Repair Company

If you encounter fraud by a credit repair company or experience any other problems, you can report the company. Since many states have laws regulating credit repair companies, if you are in one of these states, you can report the problem to your local consumer affairs office or to your state attorney general. You can also file a complaint with the FTC. Although the FTC can't resolve an individual dispute, it can take action against a company if there are enough reports showing a pattern of possible law violations. File your complaint online at www.ftc.gov/complaint or call 1-877-FTC-HELP.

CREDIT CARD INTEREST RATE REDUCTION SCAMS

Another type of credit card scam that targets mostly people with high debts and low credit scores is an offer to reduce your credit card interest rate. If you are able to pay off your credit card balance each month, the high rate doesn't matter, but if you can't, which many people with high debts can't, then a high interest rate can result in a major cost at 2 percent or more a month, 24 percent or more a year.

How the Interest Rate Reduction Scam Works

Basically, the rate reduction scam begins when a scammer contacts you by e-mail or with a prerecorded phone call claiming the company can negotiate significantly lower interest rates with your credit card issuer if you pay them a fee first. However, the FTC's Telemarketing Sales Rules state that companies that offer rate reduction or other credit-relief services are not permitted to charge you a fee before they settle or reduce your debt. The only way they can legally get any money from you in advance is for you to put the money in a dedicated bank account administered by an independent third party, who may charge a reasonable fee—with the emphasis on the word "reasonable." If the fee seems too high, that's probably a sign of a scam. In any case, the administrator of this account is responsible for transferring funds from your account after a rate reduction or debt relief occurs. If the company can't achieve these results, the money stays in your account, and eventually, if you decide to end your arrangement with the company, you get your money back.

Other scam warnings include companies that claim to have a special relationship with the credit card companies, guarantee rates that allow you to pay off your debt three to five times faster, or claim that these lower rates are only available for a limited time. Some may even offer a money-back guarantee to further entice you to use their service. Companies making these promises can't do anything for you that you can't do for yourself. As the FTC notes, you have as much influence with your credit card company as these companies do, and you are just as likely to get turned down for a rate reduction as they are. FTC investigators found that customers for these services don't get the claimed rate reductions, don't save the promised amount from their total debt, and aren't able to pay off their credit card debt three to five times faster. Additionally, they struggle to get refunds from these services, when their promises come to naught.

An Example of a Reduce-Your-Rate Scam

An example of such a credit card interest rate scam is that of Payless Solutions in Orlando, Florida, which was sued by the FTC and the Florida Attorney General for making illegal robocalls to pitch its worthless service. As a June 29, 2015, release from the FTC describes, the company, which changed its name to All Us Marketing, conducted a massive robocall campaign, with many calls directed to seniors, to get consumers to pay up front to get their interest rate reduced. In these calls, the company claimed that their program would save consumers at least $2,500 in a short time and would enable them to pay off their debts more quickly. Consumers who fell for the scheme paid between $300 and $4,999 up front for their useless services. And in some cases the company illegally charged consumers who had not agreed to these charges.

Among other things, the suit claimed that the consumers did not actually get the promised interest rate reduction or savings. Instead, as described by the FTC, "some consumers receive(d) a package of financial education information that they did not request or agree to pay for. In other cases, the defendants use(d) consumers' personal information to apply for new credit cards, presumably with low introductory interest rates, without consumers' knowledge or consent."[3] Additionally, the company made many calls to consumers whose phone numbers were on the FTC's National Do Not Call Registry, and they violated the FTC's Telemarketing Sales Rule and Florida's Telemarketing and Consumer Fraud and Abuse Act, which make it illegal to "sell products or services with out-of-the-blue robocalls."

A check of the company online indicates that it is now out of business. Its Facebook page is empty, and a review of the company by the San Diego Better Business Bureau, where it would appear the company did business for a while, indicated it is out of business. So at least that's one less scammer that consumers have to worry about.

What You Can Do to Protect Yourself

First, you can try to reduce your interest rate on credit card purchases on your own by calling the customer service phone number on the back of your card. Ask for a reduced rate and perhaps provide an incentive for the company to do this, such as saying you were thinking of buying but were holding back because of the high rate. Another approach might be that due to the high rate you are considering getting another card, but if they can reduce the rate, you will remain with the company. Perhaps also bring up your payment history if you have been paying regularly and play the loyal-customer card. If they turn you down, wait a month or so and try again—you'll undoubtedly get a different customer rep when you do, since the reps operate out of a call center. Still another strategy is to get another card with a lower interest rate, and if you have built up a good payment record with this company, you may well qualify for a card from another company with an even lower rate.

If you do get a phone call or e-mail with a reduce-your-rate offer, here are some things that the FTC recommends.

- Don't give out your credit card number and expiration date or any other information requested, such as your security number and address on the card, since if this is a scammer, he or she can use this information to charge your credit card for their own purchases or sell this information to other scammers.
- Don't provide any other personal and financial information, such as your bank account or Social Security numbers, which some scammers will ask for when they are doing an unsolicited sales pitch. They can use that information for other frauds against you, including creating a credit or debit card in your name, which they then use for their own purposes.
- Be skeptical about *any* unsolicited sales calls, especially if they are prerecorded. If you have listed your phone number on the National Do Not Call Registry, you shouldn't get any calls from telemarketers, unless you have previously done business with a company within the last eighteen months or have asked that company for information within the last three months.
- If you want to report a telemarketer calling you in violation of the Do Not Call Registry or to get your phone number on the registry, go to http://www.donotcall.com or call 1-888-382-1222 to list your phone number.

Third, if you have been a victim of a credit card interest rate reduction scam—or a scammer tried to lure you into this, you can file a complaint with the FTC at www.ftccomplaintassistant.gov or call the FTC at 1-877-FTC-HELP (1-877-382-4357).

Finally, if a rate-reduction company has charged you for a service you didn't order, authorize, or receive and you can't get a refund, contact your credit card company to dispute this by claiming fraud. Usually, your credit card company will give you the benefit of the doubt and reverse the charges. Follow up in writing with whatever information is required, as requested by your credit card company.

AUTOMATIC DEBIT SCAMS

This is still another scam that also targets individuals who have high debts and low credit scores, though variations on the scam can target others. In this case, the scammer calls you or contacts you by mail or e-mail promising you that you can qualify for a major credit card, even if you have had past credit problems. A variation on this scam is to tell you that you have won a free prize or offer you some other benefit.

How the Scam Works

Whatever the reason the scammer gives you, he or she will commonly ask you right away if you have a checking account, and once you say yes, the scammer explains a little more about the offer. Finally, the scammer will ask you to get one of your checks and read off the numbers at the bottom, which are your bank's routing number and account number. While some scammers may not tell you why the company needs this information, others may tell you they need this account to make sure you qualify for the offer. In some cases, a telemarketer may tell you quite honestly that this information is needed to debit your checking account. In any case, once the telemarketer gets this information, you are subjected to the scam. Certainly, there are times when you might actually authorize a company to take money on a regular basis from your checking account for a product or service when you expressly agree to this payment method. But in this case, a scammer is getting your information in order to get your money based on false claims of helping you get a major credit card, reduce your interest, or whatever the promise.

Another way your bank gets debited is that as soon as the company gets your checking account information, it creates a "demand draft," which is processed much like a check, with your name, account number, and amount. However, the draft does not require your signature, as does a check. Once your bank receives the draft, it takes that amount from your checking account and pays the company's bank, and you may not realize this until you get a copy of your bank statement or see it in your online transactions record.

Obtaining your bank information in this way is actually illegal. Any seller or telemarketer is required to obtain a verifiable authorization from you to obtain a payment from your bank account. In other words, they need your express permission to debit your account, and they can only get this authorization in one of three ways. First, the person has to tell you that money will be taken from your bank account as payment, not, as some scammers say, because they need this information for verification or computer purposes. Second, once you authorize payment from your bank, they must get your written authorization, tape record your authorization, or send you a written confirmation before they take money from your bank account. Should they record your authorization or use a written authorization, they must tell you, and you must receive the following information: the date and amount of the demand draft, the person or company that will receive your money (called the payee), the number of draft payments if more than one, a phone number you can call during normal business hours, and the date you are giving your verbal authorization. Finally, the seller or telemarketer has to include in the confirmation notice the procedure you can use to dispute the accuracy of this confirmation notice and get a refund. If you don't get this information, this is a sign of a scammer.

How to Protect Yourself from Being Scammed

The best way to protect yourself is not to give out your checking account number over the phone or in response to an e-mail unless you know the company and understand why the information is necessary. In particular, be suspicious of any offer to help you qualify for a major credit card or reduce your credit card interest rate or to give you a free prize or special discount. Remember that companies don't ask for your bank account information unless you have expressly agreed to pay them for some product or service in this way.

What You Can Do If You Are a Victim

As in other cases where someone is extracting payment from you without your permission or does not provide the promised service, if a company takes money from your bank without your knowledge or authorization, you can ask for a refund, and if you don't get it, that company has violated the law. Likewise, if you get a written confirmation notice that does not accurately represent your understanding of the offer you accepted, you should follow the refund procedures that they should have provided and ask for a refund. If you don't get it, that is a violation of the law too.

Once you don't get your refund in a timely manner—within three or four days of requesting it, and commonly you will also get a confirmation that the refund is being processed, consider yourself a victim of fraud and immediately contact your bank. Advise your bank that you did not authorize the debit and you want to prevent any further debiting of your account. Normally, when you report this immediately as a fraud claim, you will get back your money. Additionally, contact your state attorney general's office. If they get enough of these complaints to show a pattern of frauds, they may proceed to take criminal action and shut down the scam.

AVOIDING PAYDAY LOANS AND LOAN AGGREGATOR SCAMS

This is another type of scam that targets those who can least afford it—those struggling with credit card and other debts and who need a quick infusion of money to make a payment for something. The problem with payday loans, according to the FTC, is that many people who get them have trouble paying them off quickly. As a result, the interest due on these loans can rapidly increase, so the person now has trouble paying off this loan, as well. It's a vicious cycle where the debt mushrooms with each effort to pay off the previous debt, and dishonest companies can make the problem for the debtor even worse.

An Example of a Payday Scam Artist

For example, as described by the FTC, one company, the Payday Support Center, promised to help people who fell behind on their payday loan payments by claiming it would pay off or eliminate payday loans very quickly. Among other things, it claimed that it could negotiate interest-free payments, apply the biweekly payment to the Center to loans, and pay off or eliminate loans—through its four- to six-month program. The company even convinced some people to stop paying the companies that had previously lent them money, including their credit card companies. On top of what the person already owed for the payday loan and previous debts, the support center charged an enrollment fee and biweekly payments, which sometimes amounted to hundreds of dollars each week.

Unfortunately, victims of this program ended up even worse off than they were when they started, much like another one of these companies that claims to reduce mortgage payments but doesn't pay the lender, resulting in the victim eventually losing his or her house to foreclosure. In this case, the victims' payments didn't go to actually paying off their loans. Rather the Payment Support Center simply kept their money, and in many cases, the victims ended up owing more money in additional interest payments and late fees added to their original debt. The only thing the Support Center did was send out form letters asking the lenders to prove that the loans were legitimate, but it did nothing to pay off or eliminate the consumers' loans as promised.

Another Type of Payday Loan Scam

Another payday loan scam involves your consumer financial information being bought from third parties and used to create a fake loan agreement, deposit money into your account, and make unauthorized withdrawals—and then the whole mess contributes to lowering your credit score. That's what occurred with one scam that netted the scammers $49 million over ten months, until the FTC asked a federal district court to stop the practice and make it possible for victims to get refunds.

In this case, a lender contacted consumers and claimed they owed them money then lied about the total cost of the loan they offered to pay it off. The lender told the consumers that their total payments on their loan would be the principal plus a onetime finance charge, but they not only withdrew that charge but took out biweekly automatic payments that were only for the interest, and not the principal. So the consumers ended up making interest-only payments indefinitely on loans they had never asked for in the first place. Unfortunately, a great number of consumers fell for this scam because they weren't on top of what they actually owed to what companies, so they were tricked into thinking they had taken out loans that were actually created in their name using their bank account information to create fake loan agreements.

Obviously, the way to stay on top of such an obvious scam is to keep track of what you owe and if unexpected withdrawals start appearing in your bank account or on your debit card, check into them to make sure they are really loans you authorized.

HOW TO PROTECT YOURSELF FROM PAYDAY LOAN SCAMS

One way to protect yourself from both the high interest of payday loans and payday loan scams is to avoid such a loan if you can by considering other ways to get out of your debts. Making a budget can help. Or at least understand how payday loans work so you can obtain one from a legitimate company and use them sparingly.

First, recognize that payday loans go by a number of different names, including "cash advance loans," "check advance loans," "postdated check loans," or "deferred deposit loans." Typically, they are advertised as a way to get enough cash to keep you going until the next payday—and get it quickly. But be aware that these small, short-term loans come with a high interest rate, whether you get them from check-cashing or finance companies or other lenders.

Basically, the way the loan works is you get a cash advance secured by a personal check or paid by an electronic transfer from your checking account or debit card. For example, if you want to borrow money, you write a personal check to the lender for the amount plus the fee for borrowing the money. The lender gives you cash in the amount of your check, less the fee, and agrees to hold the check until the loan is due, usually your next payday—or if you give the company permission, they will deposit the amount you are borrowing, less the fee, directly into your checking account. Then, when the loan amount is due, the company will debit your debit card or bank account directly. In the event you can't pay the full amount or can only pay part of it on the due date, the lender can roll over the loan but will add an additional fee for the additional amount you borrow. Should you need a series of these loans, the amounts due can become astronomical. For instance, you have to pay 15 percent, or $15, for a $100 loan for two weeks; if you have to borrow three more times, you are paying $60, or 60 percent, for borrowing that money, and over a year, the annual percentage rate is 391 percent.

So these loans can be hugely expensive, even though they are legal. However, where the scam comes in is if the lender does not tell you the true cost of borrowing the money. According to the federal Truth in Lending Act, a payday loan is regarded like any type of credit, whereby the lender has to disclose the cost of the loan. Therefore, the payday lender has to give you the finance charge (the dollar amount) and the annual percentage rate (APR, which is the cost of credit on a yearly basis) in writing before you sign for the loan. This APR is based on the amount you are borrowing, the interest rate, any credit costs you are charged, and the length of your loan. But if the company doesn't give you the full picture of what you are paying, it is illegal, and you should avoid a loan from such a company.

Considering Alternatives to Payday Loans

Since payday loans are so expensive and they can further damage your credit if you pay late or don't pay, you should look into alternatives to such loans, even from a legitimate company. Some of the alternatives the FTC recommends are these:

- See if you can get a small loan from your credit union or a small loan company. You might also be able to get a cash advance on a credit card, although it may have a higher interest rate than other sources of funds. Shop around to learn what is available, find out the terms, and compare the offers before you decide.

- Look for the credit offer with the lowest cost by comparing the APR and finance charge, which includes the loan fees, interest, and other credit costs.
- If you are having trouble with making payments, ask for more time from your creditor or loan servicer as quickly as possible. Many may be willing to work with you if they believe you are acting in good faith, such as by extending the due date of your bills. Find out what charges you might incur, however, such as a late charge, additional finance charge, or higher interest rate, to decide if this is the best alternative.
- If you need help working out a debt repayment plan with creditors or creating a budget, contact a local consumer credit counseling service. Many nonprofit groups throughout the United States offer this assistance for no or low cost, and if you are contemplating a bankruptcy, such credit counseling is usually required as one of the steps to a bankruptcy filing. You might also find counseling help by checking with your employer, credit union, or housing authority.
- Make a realistic budget to keep down your expenses, and avoid unnecessary purchases, such as small everyday items, like a cup of coffee, because those costs can add up. If you can build up some savings, even with small deposits, you will have some funds to tide you over in emergencies, rather than borrowing at a high rate of interest.
- Ask if you have or your bank offers overdraft or bounce protection on your checking account; this feature can help to reduce fees from individual overdrafts from checks or electronic withdrawals. In some cases, overdraft protection is tied to a separate savings account, so the money is taken from that. But at least that will save you the high fees (generally about $35) for a bounced check.

In sum, try to avoid payday loans if you can, and if you use one, borrow as little as possible. Also, the FTC advises to borrow no more than you can afford to pay off with your next paycheck and still have enough to make it to the next payday. And it goes without saying—avoid payday scammers who don't tell you the real cost of taking out a payday loan.

LOAN AGGREGATOR SCAMS

Still another type of come-on that could be a scam is an offer from a loan aggregator. These companies are not so much offering you a loan as collecting information from you as leads and then selling the information you provide on your loan application to a third party. This application includes all sorts of personal and financial information, including your name, address, phone number, birth date, Social Security number, bank or credit card account number, and annual income. In fact, some aggregators, like many fraudsters, use keystroke loggers, which is software that records what you type. So even if you don't actually submit the application after you fill it out, say because you change your mind about applying for the loan, the aggregator may still have some or all of your information, which it can sell or use to access your bank account or credit card or for identity theft.

One of the big problems is that you might think you are dealing directly with a lender to get a loan, but in fact you are dealing with a loan aggregator, who acts a middleman, like a broker that obtains your personal and financial information on your loan application and then looks for a lender who might give you a loan. This is like when you apply for a credit card with a bank, who then submits your application to the credit card company for an approval, or when you go to an insurance agent who represents a number of auto insurance, home insurance, or health insurance companies.

Certainly, many of these loan aggregators are legit, just like brokers in other industries. But some are not, as selling personal and financial information has become a business. So you may find that a loan aggregator might sell your information to companies who try to sell you goods or services, or worse, charge you for goods you didn't agree to buy. And then that charge could appear on your credit card or as a deduction from your bank account.

That's what one company, Ideal Financial, did, earning over $25 million in fraudulent charges. As the FTC describes, the company debited consumers' bank and credit card accounts without their authorization, and if a consumer complained, Ideal Financial advised them that they had bought financial management or consulting services at a payday loan website where they gave their bank account numbers with the understanding that, upon approval, the lender would deposit the loan directly into their bank account. Ideal Financial then put through the unapproved charges, and, since their offer appealed to consumers who were already struggling financially, these charges sometimes resulted in expensive bank penalty and overdraft fees for some victims.

To avoid being victimized by such a company, be cautious before you give out any personal or financial information and know who you are dealing with to make sure this is a reputable company. More specifically, the FTC recommends the following:

- Unless you have initiated the contact or know the company or individual you are dealing with, don't give out your personal information on the phone, via e-mail or regular mail, or on a website.
- Regularly check your bank statement and credit card bills, and if there are any charges you don't recognize call to find out who these are from, and dispute any charges you don't recognize; claim fraud if you believe the company put through unauthorized charges.
- If you get an e-mail from a company claiming to have an account with you and asking for personal information, don't click on any links, since this could be from a fraudster seeking such information. Instead, type the company name into your Web browser, visit their site, and contact them through customer service. Or call the customer service number on your monthly account statement. In either case, ask if the company really did send you a request for personal information. If not, this could well be a scam.
- If you see an ad or get an offer that appeals to you, before you give out any information, check out the company behind it. To find out if the company is legit or not, you can do an online search and add in the term "review," "complaint," or "scam" in the search box. If you do find bad reviews, complaints, or scam reports, that's a sign to stay away. Likewise, if you can't find contact information for the company, that's a warning to stay away, too.
- Even if an ad appears on a reputable site, such as Yahoo or Facebook, that doesn't mean it is from a reputable company, since these sites commonly accept ads from whoever pays for the ad and aren't able to check out or endorse most ads. So check out the company just as you would in getting an offer from that company directly.

- Check out a company's privacy policies, and be cautious if the site provides information to third parties, since that could mean they can give out your personal and financial information to anyone. If you can, opt out of any offers that indicate the company can share your information with third parties, and if you can't opt out, check with the company about who they share your information with. Should you feel uncomfortable with these plans for sharing, don't do business with the company.

CREDIT CARD LOSS PROTECTION SCAMS

An offer of credit card loss protection is another scam; you don't need it. The law limits your liability to $50 for unauthorized charges—and if you are claiming fraud, you may have no liability for the charges at all.

Generally, the way the scam works is you will get a call or e-mail indicating that you need this insurance because the law has changed, so people are liable for all unauthorized charges on their account. This is not true, so any credit card loss protection or insurance programs are worthless, according to the FTC. Instead, don't pay for any unauthorized charges and simply file a claim that you are disputing a charge with your credit card company or bank and follow their procedures for doing so.

As the FTC advises, these protection offers are designed to take advantage of consumers' uncertainty about the law with false claims about the need for this protection insurance. Among some of the false claims they may make are these:

- You are liable for over $50 in unauthorized charges on your credit or debit card.
- You need this protection because "computer hackers can access your credit card number and charge thousands of dollars to your account."
- This insurance will protect you, because a computer bug could enable scammers to place unauthorized charges on your credit card or debit card.

- The caller or e-mail sender is from the credit card company's "security department," and they want to "activate the protection feature on your credit card."

As previously noted, you should not give out your personal and financial information, including your credit card or bank account numbers over the phone or online unless you are familiar with the individual or company asking for it, and you are sure that this really is the person a caller claims to be. Otherwise, once scammers have your information, they can use it to charge your card, deduct money from your account, open a credit card in your name, or commit other types of identity theft fraud.

ADVANCE-FEE LOAN SCAMS

The advance-fee loan scam is one where the lender asks for payment of a fee before granting the loan. It typically affects consumers looking for a loan or credit card but have trouble qualifying because of their poor credit history. These consumers may be drawn by ads and websites that guarantee them loans or credit cards, regardless of credit history. It can seem like a wonderful opportunity. But no legitimate lender can guarantee or suggest that you are likely to get a loan or credit card before you apply.

There are certain signs to look for that indicate that an advance-fee loan offer is probably a scam, according to the FTC.

- The lender doesn't care about your credit history, and has an ad that says something like: "Bad credit? No problem," "We don't care about your past. You deserve a loan," or "No hassle—guaranteed."
- The lender doesn't clearly or prominently disclose the fees. It says you've been approved for the loan, but then asks for money from you before granting it. The lender may claim the fee is just for "insurance," "processing," or "paperwork," but whatever the claim, if the lender seeks any up-front fee, walk away. While legitimate lenders commonly charge application, appraisal, or credit report fees, they clearly and prominently indicate their fees and

they take the fees from the amount you borrow, not up front. In fact, any fees are usually paid to the lender or broker *after* the loan is approved. Moreover, if such a lender assures you they won't check your credit history but asks for personal information, such as your Social Security number or bank account number, that is a sign they might use this information to debit your bank account to pay a hidden fee.

- The lender offers you a loan on the phone, since it is illegal for companies to promise you a loan or credit card and ask you to pay for it.
- The lender uses a name that sounds like that of a well-known or respected organization and has a professional-looking website with this name. That could be a scam, because some fraudsters have pretended to be the Better Business Bureau, a major bank, or other respected organizations. Some even create forged paperwork or pay people to be references for them. Thus, you should get the company's phone number from the phone book, directory assistance, or doing an online search. Then call to see if the company is really who they say they are. Also, get the company's physical address, since if the company has a P.O. box, it's a warning sign that it isn't a legitimate company, and you should do further research to check them out, such as calling the Better Business Bureau in their area—or checking their name with "scam," "review," or "complaint" in a search engine.
- The lender is not registered in your state. Lenders and loan brokers have to register in any states where they do business. To check, you can call your state attorney general's office or your state's Department of Banking or Financial Regulation. If they are not registered, it is a sign of a scammer.
- The lender asks you to wire money or pay an individual. A legitimate lender will never ask you to do that. Moreover, don't send money orders or use a wire transfer service for a loan, since you can't do much if you lose money this way. In fact, wire transfers are often used to send money to someone who is out of state or out of the country, which an advance fee scammer might well be.

REFUND AND RECOVERY SCAMS

Still another scam is one where the scammer promises to get the consumer a refund or recover money lost in a previous scam. The way they know about you is that the scammers buy and sell what are called "sucker lists," which have the names of people who have already lost money in response to a fraudulent scheme in the past. If you were a patsy once, the thinking goes, you will be again.

Accordingly, the scammers call you promising that they will recover the money you lost or any prize or merchandise you didn't receive. But the catch is you have to pay a fee in advance, which is against the law, since under the Telemarketing Sales Rule, callers cannot ask for or accept payment from you until seven business days after you receive the money or other item they recover from you.

When the scammer calls, you might not even know you have been scammed by some fraudulent promotion, such as by providing your personal information or paying money to participate in a phony prize promotion, charity drive, or business opportunity. But if you have, the scammers have your name and contact information, including how much money you have spent in the past on phony offers. That can give the fraudster an idea of how much money you might be willing to pay in a refund and recovery scam.

Once the scammers have stated their initial lie that they will recover the money you lost or the prize or product you didn't receive for a fee, they may embellish their promise with additional lies to make their initial lie seem more credible. For instance, they may claim they represent a reputable company or a government agency; they may say they are already holding money for you; they may offer to file the required complaint paperwork with companies or government agencies on your behalf so you don't have to spend your valuable time doing this. And some may claim they get a company or government agency to put your name at the top of a list for reimbursements to victims.

But it's all lies, and you shouldn't believe it when anyone calls saying they can recover money, merchandise, or prizes you never received and asks you for an advance fee.

Should someone claim to represent a government agency that recovers any of these things for you, report them to the FTC, because national, state, and local consumer protection agencies and nonprofit organizations do not charge for their services.

Additionally, the FTC recommends that before you use any company to provide a refund or recovery service, ask what specific services the company provides and the cost of each service. Get the company to provide this information in writing, too—and it is likely that a scammer won't do this. Also, you might check whether this a legitimate company with your local law enforcement and consumer agencies by asking whether other people have registered any complaints about the company. You can also search online for the company name combined with the terms: "complaint" and "scam," as previously noted, to see if there have been reported problems with the company.

Don't give out your credit card, debit card, or checking account numbers in response to a company offer to recover your money or secure a refund for you. This could be just another way to not only get your money but get personal and financial information from you that can be used in other scams and by other scammers.

DISPUTING BILLS FOR MERCHANDISE YOU NEVER RECEIVED AND BILLING ERRORS

Sometimes if you don't receive merchandise and are billed for or want to get a refund, there is a legitimate reason, such as an error in shipping or billing, and you can correct this in various ways yourself. You don't need to rely on a third party who might well be a scammer, although a legitimate company may save you the hassle, as long as they don't get paid until you get your merchandise or your refund.

You are actually protected under two federal laws. One is the Mail, Internet, or Telephone Order Merchandise Rule; the other is the Fair Credit Billing Act. They provide various procedures for you to follow if you order merchandise and don't get it or encounter a billing problem. But the first step is to contact the seller to try to resolve the problem and either get the merchandise or service you ordered or get a refund. Below are the steps to follow for credit card purchases according to the FTC, which may differ for debit cards. While a debit card may act like a credit card, there are actually more protections with a credit card, though some debit card issuers may voluntarily offer you help in resolving problems when you don't get merchandise you bought with a debit card.

Disputing a Credit Card Billing

If you can't resolve this directly with the seller, then it is possible you are dealing with a case of fraud where you are promised certain merchandise but don't receive it or the merchandise isn't as advertised. In either case, you have to show that you have been defrauded and that this is more than a run-of-the-mill misunderstanding. Some of this advice will apply to any kind of dispute, though the focus here is on a dispute where you believe there is a credit card fraud.

As the FTC points out, many sellers are not supposed to charge a credit card before they ship something or provide the service according to the policies of many credit card companies, although an exception might be when you agree to pay a retainer for a service or an advance fee for a product that is made especially for you. However, if you think a seller has inappropriately charged your account too soon, you can report it to your credit card company so the company knows the seller isn't following its policies.

To dispute a billing error with your company or if you were billed for merchandise you didn't receive, the FTC recommends writing to the credit card company at its address for billing inquiries, which is different from the address for sending your payments. Include your name, address, account number, and a description of the billing error. A template for a sample letter suggested by the FTC, looks like this:

[Date]

[Your Name] [Your Address] [Your City, State, Zip Code] [Your Account Number]

[Name of Creditor] [Billing Inquiries] [Address] [City, State, Zip Code]

Dear Sir or Madam:

I am writing to dispute a billing error in the amount of [$_____] on my account. The amount is inaccurate because [describe the problem]. I am requesting that the error be corrected, that any finance and other charges related to the disputed amount be credited as well, and that I receive an accurate statement.

Enclosed are copies of [use this sentence to describe any information you are enclosing, like sales slips or payment records] supporting my position. Please investigate this matter and correct the billing error as soon as possible.

Sincerely,
[Your name]

Enclosures: [List the enclosures]

Send your letter to reach the credit card company within sixty days after the incorrect billing was first mailed to you. Ideally, send your letter by certified mail and ask for a return receipt so you have proof of what you send the credit card company. Include copies of sales slips and other documents that support your position, and keep a copy of your dispute letter.

The credit card company has to acknowledge your complaint in writing within thirty days after receiving it unless the problem has been resolved. The credit card company is supposed to resolve the dispute within two billing cycles, but not more than ninety days after it gets your letter.

You are permitted to withhold payment on the amount you dispute and any related charges during the investigation, though you have to pay any part of the bill that you don't question, including any finance charges on the undisputed amount.

If the company has already charged you for a product, but production or shipping is delayed, there may be some flexibility in when you have to file your dispute, especially if you didn't expect to be charged by the seller before the merchandise was shipped. But as soon as you are aware there could be a problem in getting what you ordered in a timely way, advise your credit card company accordingly.

If in pursuing this dispute you feel the seller or service provider is not acting in good faith, then you can claim a fraud, and at this point, as long as you can provide some evidence of what you ordered and expected and what you didn't receive, your credit card company will usually give you the benefit of the doubt.

Disputing a Debit Card Charge

The consumer protections for a debit card are a little different from credit card protections, although some debit cards are issued through credit card providers, such as when you have a MasterCard or Visa issued by a bank. In some cases, according to the FTC, you may not be able to dispute a debit from your bank and get a refund for nondelivery or late delivery. However, some debit card issuers may voluntarily offer to provide you with a refund if you didn't get the merchandise you purchased with a debit card. And if you are claiming fraud, debit card providers or your bank will generally provide you with a full refund.

Cancelling Orders and Getting a Refund When You Shop by Mail

If you decide to cancel an order for a good reason, such as if the seller can't ship by the time advertised and you don't accept the delay (and advise the seller accordingly if the delay is less than thirty days), the seller is supposed to give you a refund within seven days after you cancel the order if you pay by cash, check, debit card, money order, or non-seller credit card. If you pay with a credit card issued by the seller, then the seller must credit your account within one billing cycle. If you do cancel and don't get your refund, after you first contact the seller to try to resolve the problem, then you can contact your credit card or bank, as appropriate about the refund you didn't get. It is in this situation where you might potentially have a fraud claim. If you can't get the matter resolved otherwise, then claim fraud, and usually you will get your money back very soon after that. Unfortunately, if you pay by cash, money order, or the seller's own credit card, you may be out of luck, since you have no one to appeal to if claiming fraud.

DEBT REDUCTION AND SETTLEMENT SCAMS

This is another scam targeting low-income individuals struggling with debts—or anyone who has gone way over their budget. The basic offer made by these companies, which may handle other kinds of credit card and dispute services, is that they can negotiate with your creditors so you can pay a "settlement" to resolve your debt, generally by paying less than what you owe.

The basic premise is perfectly sound. You took on a certain amount of debt thinking you could make enough to pay it off, but due to changed circumstances, you now can't, so you want to negotiate a lower amount. The creditor may believe your story and agree to this, fearing to end up getting paid nothing. On the other hand, the creditor may feel you can pay but don't want to and are making up excuses. It is into this scenario that a company that reduces and settles credit card debt comes into the picture and offers to handle the negotiations for you.

This basic premise is absolutely fine. Creditors and debtors work out these kinds of settlements everyday—and without any breaking of legs, to note a popular movie theme. Even the federal government has an offer and compromise program, and so does the state, along with hardship waivers to stop collection efforts for six months to a year while a debtor gets back on his or her feet.

But suppose you feel more comfortable having someone else negotiate your debt for you. That's where these companies offering to reduce or settle your credit card or other debts come in. There are legitimate companies that do this, but the scammers can take advantage of this process by engaging in deception and making claims they can't fulfill. Or worse, they charge you a fee before they resolve any debts instead of making a deduction, as they can legally, from what you collect. So that you can distinguish the scammers from the real deal, as well as weigh the risks of working with a legitimate debt settlement company, following are some details about how the debt settlement process works and when to suspect a scam.

How the Debt Settlement Process Works

Typically, a debt settlement company acts on your behalf to negotiate with your creditors so you can pay a "settlement" or lump-sum amount to resolve your debt and pay less than the full amount you owe. In order to make this payment, the company asks you to set aside a certain amount of money each month in an escrow-like account until you accumulate enough savings to pay off the settlement. These companies will commonly ask you to stop making any monthly payments to your creditors on the theory that this might undermine the settlement process. However, while a legitimate debt settlement company may be able to settle one or more of your debts, there are certain risks associated with these programs, so consider them before you decide you want to sign up with such a company. According to the FTC, the key risks are these:

- It can take three years or more for your debts to actually be settled, since these programs often require you to deposit money into a special savings account during this time until all or at least some of the debts are settled. Due to this long time period many people drop out. So before you decide to sign up for such a program, make sure you can financially handle setting aside the required monthly amount for the program. Also, consider the possibility that you could encounter obstacles along the way that might disrupt your plans to pay off a debt.
- Your creditors aren't required to agree to negotiate to settle your debt. So the debt settlement company might not be able to settle some of your debts, even if you are setting aside the monthly amount required. Commonly, these companies try to negotiate your smaller debts first, so the interest and fees on the larger debts could grow in the meantime.
- Since these debt settlement programs often ask or encourage you to stop sending payments directly to your creditors, your credit report may suffer and there may be other negative effects. For instance, as the FTC points out, the late fees and penalties on your debts can still accumulate, so you have even more debts. You could even get calls from your creditors or debt collectors representing them asking you to pay. Some creditors could even sue you to get their money—and sometimes when creditors win, they may garnish your wages or put a lien on your house.

Still another consideration is that the money you are spending on the program, which includes the fee for settling each debt, is money that could instead go toward paying down the debt, although the negotiating company might have more skill and save you the hassle of directly dealing with your creditors to seek a reduced payment or payment plan.

Given these risks, why even consider a debt settlement program? Because they do sometimes work, and they do enable someone else to negotiate for you. They may also be able to stave off some debtors, since you are participating in a debt repayment program, which shows your good faith in trying to pay your creditors.

Avoiding the Debt Settlement Scammers

Besides the risks of working with a legitimate company, another problem of participating in a debt settlement program is that there are a number of scams out there where companies offering these programs may deceive with false promises and not deliver the debt relief. As the FTC warns, they may promise that they can settle all of your credit card debts for 30–60 percent of what you owe, when such a result is not guaranteed. Some companies may try to collect a fee for their service up front before they have settled any of your debts—but these advance fees are prohibited by the FTC's Telemarketing Sales Rules. Some companies may also fail to explain the risks associated with a debt settlement program, which are those outlined above—namely that many or most consumers drop out without settling their debts, that your credit report could suffer, or that debt collectors may still call you, though you are in the program.

Accordingly, the FTC advises that you should avoid entering a debt settlement program with a company that does any of the following:

- charges any fees before settling your debts (which is illegal)
- claims there is a new government program to bail out personal credit card debt (because there is no such program)
- guarantees it can make your unsecured debt go away or pay it off for pennies on the dollar (it can't do either)
- tells you to stop communicating with your creditors (which a legitimate company may also advise) but doesn't explain the consequences of doing so (which you should know before you sign up for such a program)
- tells you it can stop all debt collection calls and lawsuits (it can't).

Aside from the obvious warning signs of fraud, it also helps to research any company you are considering hiring to handle a debt settlement program for you. Some of the things to do include the following, also based on the advice of the FTC:

- Check out the company with your state attorney general and local consumer protection agency to learn if any consumer complaints are on file about this company. Additionally, ask your state attorney general if the company has to be licensed to work in the state, and if so, if it is.
- Check out the company by entering its name with the word "complaints" or "scam" in a search engine, which will turn up other comments about the companies, including news about any lawsuits by state or federal regulators for engaging in deceptive or unfair practices.

What to Expect from a Legitimate Debt Settlement Company

When you do work with a legitimate debt settlement company, you can expect to have to enter into certain agreements, which may sound like you are giving the company a ticket to defraud you. But those arrangements are how these companies operate, so you should expect the following to occur if you do sign up for a debt settlement program:

- You may have to put money in a dedicated bank account administered by an independent third party. These funds should remain yours and you should get any interest that accrues. The account administrator is also permitted to charge you a reasonable fee for maintaining your account, and he or she takes care of transferring funds from your account to pay your creditors an agreed-upon settlement amount as well as the fee to the debt settlement company for arranging for the settlement.
- The debt settlement company can only charge you a proportion of its full fee for each debt it settles, based on a percentage of the amount you save through the settlement. It has to tell you both the percentage it charges and the estimated dollar amount it expects to save you. In effect, this is like paying a contingency fee to a lawyer who helps you win a case.

- The debt settlement company has to make a full disclosure to you about its program. This disclosure should include its fees and terms and conditions of its services. It should also tell you how long it will take to get results, which means telling you how many months or years it will take before it can make an offer to each creditor to settle your debt. And remember, this is a long-haul program, because it will take time for your savings to build up enough to pay off one or more creditors. Additionally, the company has to tell you how much money or what percentage of each outstanding debt you have to save in the dedicated bank account set up for you before it will make an offer to each creditor for you. For example, it might tell you that you have to save $1,000 before it will offer one creditor $500 on a $800 debt and another creditor $300 on a $700 debt. The extra money in your account provides some extra funds for negotiating, but the creditor has to agree to accept a significantly lower amount.

- The debt settlement company has to advise you of the possible negative consequences if it asks you or depends on you to stop making payments to your creditors, such as the possible damage to your credit score, the possibility that your creditors may sue you or continue with the collection process, and that your credit card company may charge you additional fees and interest.

- Finally the debt settlement company must tell you that the funds in the bank are yours and you are entitled to any interest earned, that the account administrator is not affiliated with the company and doesn't get any referral fees (if it did, this could provide a basis for a fraudulent connection), and that you can withdraw your money at any time without penalty (if you can't, that's another fraud alert). In short, if the program works as it should, you should be able to walk away when you want to without any consequences if the company hasn't made any settlements to reduce your debts.

One more thing to consider is that any savings you get from a debt relief service can be considered taxable income, and your creditors, including credit card companies, may report your settled debt to the IRS, so you may end up with some taxes unless your total debts are more than the fair market value of your assets. A debt settlement company should not be giving tax advice unless the company owner or adviser is also a certified tax professional. However, though the company may not be able to give you specific advice, they can explain that there are tax consequences of reducing your debts, so you should talk to a tax professional to find out what the tax consequences are of saving money on paying your debts.

An Example of a Debt Relief Scammer

Not only do you have to be careful to avoid the debt settlement scammers and recognize the real consequences of participating in a debt settlement program, but you have to avoid the crafty imitators, who may cloak themselves in symbols of credibility but aren't what they seem. An example of this is one San Antonio–based lead generator, Christopher Mallett, who created the "Consumer Services Protection Commission" website, which purported to be a national consumer protection agency that was designed to help the consumer "avoid fraud, deception, and/or unfair business practices in the financial assistance marketplace." Then, the site described the agency's role in enforcing the law and educating consumers about how to "spot and avoid fraud and deception." It even included a blue and gold logo with the scales of justice.

But in fact the site was used to deceive and defraud customers who were having difficulty paying their bills. Then, like reeling in fish on a line, he referred those he hooked to companies that sold mortgage, tax, and debt relief services with a promise that they could reduce or eliminate the individual's debt. Moreover, Mallett further deceived consumers by creating another fictitious agency, the U.S. Mortgage Relief Counsel, with a website that included a picture of the U.S. Capitol and a promise that the service would direct consumers to "officials licensed with the National Mortgage Licensing Service." But neither Mallett nor any of his sites were affiliated with the FTC or any other government agency. He was just claiming the affiliation to deceive individuals to use his services.

Plus, besides claiming these false affiliations, he used false or unsubstantiated claims that people who responded to his offer had their debts substantially reduced. For instance, one of his success stats charts showed that people's debts were settled for only 16–40 percent of the amount owed.

Accordingly, the FTC, with the assistance of the Tennessee Attorney General, filed a lawsuit in federal court in Washington, D.C., against Mallett for his deceptive practices.

DEALING WITH CHIP CARD SCAMS

Finally, even though the new credit and debit chip cards are designed to reduce fraud, including counterfeiting, by providing a unique transaction number for every transaction, the scammers are already at work to find new ways to scam the millions of consumers who haven't gotten a chip card. And of course, the scammers can always steal your card or get the personal information from you to make online purchases and charges in your name, since the chip cards only provide the extra protection when you actually use it in person with a merchant who has the new equipment to scan a chip card. So if only about 30 percent of the merchants have this equipment and 30 percent of consumers have and are using these cards, you can see where there is only partial protection for using these cards. Add in the growing use of online purchasing, and you can see where chip cards are not yet the major solution to credit card fraud.

And then there's the pitch scammers use with those who don't have a card. As described by the FTC, scammers are e-mailing people claiming to be their card issuer. They then claim that they need you to update your account information so they can issue you a new chip card. All you have to do is to update your account by confirming some personal information or clicking a link to continue the process. If you do reply with personal information, you are opening yourself up to identity theft. And if you click on a link you may additionally install a malware program on your device, which can steal your personal information, send you spam, monitor your online activity, cause your computer or other device to crash, and use any information about you to commit fraud.

To tell if the e-mail is from a scammer, look for these warning signs, according to the FTC:

- Your credit card or debit card company has no reason to contact you by e-mail or by phone to confirm your personal information before sending you a new chip card. Therefore, don't respond to any e-mail or call that asks for your card number. Normally, your credit card or debit card company will simply send you the new card by mail and ask you to call the number on back of the card to confirm and activate it.

- To further verify that this is a scam, you can call your credit card company at the number on your card to ask about the e-mail or call you received.
- Don't click on a link in an e-mail to provide personal information. Only provide this information on a company's website and only if you type the Web address yourself and see an indication that the site is secure, such as a URL that begins with "https," since the "s" means the site is secure.

7

PROTECTING YOUR CREDIT CARD

Another type of fraud can occur when your credit card is lost or stolen, or you have given your card or your card number to someone who has used it to make unauthorized transactions.

YOUR BASIC PROTECTIONS IF YOUR CARD OR CARD NUMBER IS LOST OR STOLEN

If your credit, ATM, or debit cards are lost or stolen, you are protected under two Federal acts: the Fair Credit Billing Act (FCBA) and the Electronic Fund Transfer Act (EFTA). The protections are slightly different if you have a credit card or an ATM/debit card, but basically you are not responsible for any transactions or charges you didn't authorize if you report the card being lost or stolen before it is used.

If someone does use your credit card before you report it stolen, your maximum liability is $50 under the FCBA, though your liability is slightly different under the EFTA, depending on how quickly you report the loss or theft. If you report it within two business days after you learn of the loss or theft, your maximum liability is also $50; but if you report it two to sixty days after you get your statement, your liability is up to $500. And if you report it more than sixty days after you get your statement, then you are responsible for any money taken from your bank account and any accounts linked to your debit account.

On the other hand, if your credit card number is stolen, though you still have your card, you are not responsible for any unauthorized use. If someone uses your debit card number, but you still have the card, you are not responsible if you report it within sixty days of getting your statement.

While the details may sound a little complicated, the basic message is clear. Keep track of your cards and report your card lost or stolen as soon as you discover it. Also, check your online credit card or bank account statement at least once every two days, or ideally once a day, so you can see if any unauthorized transactions appear, and if so, report them immediately.

You will also get some help from the fraud department of your credit card company or bank, in that they will be looking for any unusual transactions, and may call you or put a hold on your account until you call them and verify by answering some questions about your account that you are you. For instance, if you travel to another country, state, or even to a distant part of your own state, the credit card company or bank may decline any new charges until you call them to explain where you are and that you have authorized the previous few charges. Commonly, they will ask you to state how much those purchases were for and when and where you made them, and they may ask some additional questions about your account, such as the answer to one or more of your security questions, such as your first car or pet's name. Only then will they release your card. This can be embarrassing when you have made a purchase and suddenly find a card is declined and you have to take five or ten minutes to verify everything on the phone, but it's good to know that your credit card company or bank is looking out for you, and if you have another credit card, that might work. You can avoid this problem by calling your credit card or bank in advance to inform them of your travel plans. Or you can get travelers' checks at your bank to take with you for distant travels.

Another scenario that could alert the fraud department at your bank or credit card company and result in a card decline is if you make one purchase at a particular place and then make another soon after that above a certain amount. Still another possibility is if you normally use your card for small purchases but then try to use it for a much bigger purchase. Sometimes a single large purchase may trigger the hold, or the second large purchase might be what does it. In effect, your credit card company or bank's fraud department has a kind of scale on which it weighs a list of possible warning signs of a fraud, and then this triggers an alert resulting in a hold on your card until you call in to clear the card. Most of the time, once you call and satisfy the fraud department that you are really you and you have made the questioned purchases, they will clear the card immediately, so you can use it again right away.

WHAT TO DO IF YOU HAVE A LOSS OR THEFT

Sometimes it's not clear when a card went missing due to a loss or theft. You may not be sure if you simply misplaced it, dropped it in the street, or left it where you made your last purchase. This is quite different from knowing your card has been taken from a purse or briefcase or that someone broke into your house or car and took your card.

If you aren't sure, take some time to see if you have simply lost your card and can find it. Once you report your card missing, it will take several days to get a new one, and, unless you have another card you can use, this can be a major inconvenience. A good way to do this is to think back to when you last saw or used your card and then imagine what you did after that. Look in those places or call the places where you were to see if someone might have found your card. If so, go get your card back as soon as possible, to reduce the chances it might go missing from whoever now has your card. But if your search proves futile after an hour or two, then quickly report the loss to reduce the chances that anyone might use your card to make unauthorized purchases. Once you report it, the usual protections kick in, depending on whether this is a credit or an ATM/debit card and how soon you reported it. In the case of a theft, likewise report it as soon as you know.

By acting quickly, you limit your liability for unauthorized charges. Plus, in the case of a theft, your quick report could help the police catch a criminal, since they can note the area where a theft has occurred and can monitor that area more closely. So you not only help yourself but also might help others in your community.

HOW TO REPORT YOUR THEFT OR LOSS

Once you are ready to report your theft or loss, call your credit card company or bank's fraud alert hotline. Generally, this will be a twenty-four-hour toll-free number. You are not liable for any unauthorized transactions that occur after your report.

The FTC says you should take these additional steps:

- Send a follow-up letter or e-mail to your credit card company or bank with your account number, date and time when you noticed your card was missing or stolen, and when you reported this.
- Check your card or bank statement regularly to see if there are any transactions that you didn't make. If so, report any of these transactions to your credit card company or bank as quickly as you can by phone and additionally send a follow-up letter to the address on your statement for billing errors.
- Normally, your credit card company or bank will take care of any liability for transactions that occur after you report the loss or hold you responsible for only $50 if you report the loss or theft within two days. But just in case, to avoid any further liability, the FTC recommends that you check if your homeowner or renter's insurance policy covers any liability for card thefts. If not, some insurance companies may allow you to change your policy to include this protection, although it is not clear that you actually need this coverage, in light of the FCBA and EFTA protections, as long as you quickly report any theft or card loss.

PROTECTING YOUR CARDS AND ACCOUNT INFORMATION ON A DAY-TO-DAY BASIS

Aside from someone simply using your lost or stolen card to make purchases, there is always the potential that your name and number can be used for identity theft, whether a fraudster has your physical card or not, and you'll find information about what to do as an identity theft victim in chapter 9. However, there are various steps you can take to reduce the chances of someone obtaining either your card or your account number. Here are some basic steps to take, many of them suggested by the FTC.

- Carry only the cards you need so if you lose your wallet, purse, or cardholder, you won't lose everything, and may still have cards you can use while any lost or stolen cards are replaced.
- If you have an ATM or debit card, keep your PIN number secure. Preferably, remember it so you don't have to write your number on anything you carry with you. In particular, don't write this number on your card or carry this number in your wallet, purse, or pocket, where a thief can easily steal it and use it. Likewise, don't write your PIN number on a deposit slip, envelope, or other papers you might easily lose or throw away.
- Retrieve your card quickly after you make a purchase so a clerk or someone in line behind you can't see your number. Likewise, don't leave your card on the counter while you are waiting to make a purchase.
- Keep your account information confidential. Don't leave it out where someone can see it or write it down.
- Don't leave yourself open to charges or overcharges when you make a purchase. To avoid unauthorized charges, don't sign a blank charge or debit slip. And to avoid overcharges, draw a line through any blank spaces above or below the total on a charge or debit slip so someone can't change the total.
- Keep good records so you know what you charged on what account. In particular, save your receipts so you can check them against your monthly statements. Then, when your monthly statements arrive in the mail or are available online, check them promptly and compare them to your receipts. If you see any mistakes or discrepancies, report them right away.
- Keep a record of all your account numbers, expiration dates, and credit or debit card companies so you have this information readily available if you need to report a loss or theft.
- Tear up or shred any receipts or old statements that have your account information to protect against fraudsters who look for such discarded information in the trash.
- When your cards expire, cut them up and make sure to cut through the account number so no one can use your card or your

account number, which could still work with a later expiration date.

- Regularly check your bank statement and online transactions to see if there are any suspicious purchases or transfers of funds. With a debit or ATM card, these transactions can appear right away; credit card transactions will take a day or two to appear. In any case, as soon as you see any discrepancies or unauthorized transactions, quickly report them to your credit card company or bank.

- Don't disclose your account number to others unless you know who they are and you have agreed to let them charge your card for a particular purpose. Be especially cautious when you speak to someone on the phone unless this is someone you already know or you initiated the call—or they are returning a call that you initiated.

- Be cautious when you respond to an ad placed by someone you don't know if this is not from an established business. For example, if you respond to an ad on Craig's List to buy something, the seller will be unlikely to take a check because the person doesn't know you either. Thus, it is safer to use cash (assuming you are making this purchase in a safe place and are not likely to be a victim of a robbery) than to give someone your credit card information. The same caution goes for making a purchase at a flea market. Unless this is an established seller, you really don't know who this person is, and it could be a setup to get credit card information from unsuspecting people who think they are just making an inexpensive purchase.

DEALING WITH UNAUTHORIZED CHARGES WHEN YOU GIVE YOUR CARD TO SOMEONE

Another potential for fraud can occur if you give your card to someone, such as a family member, friend, business associate, or employee to make purchases for you. For example, you are ill and you give your card to a trusted friend who is helping you out by acting as a caregiver. Another situation might be when you ask someone at work to do some shopping errands for you. Or perhaps you want to get tickets for a show and a friend offers to get them for you.

Such cases happen all the time and usually there is no problem. The person gets what you want, gives you a receipt for what was purchased, and all is fine. But sometimes things go wrong; the person loses the card or claims it was stolen or the person buys something you did not authorize. In some cases, such unexpected charges could result from a misunderstanding about what the person was authorized to do with the card, but in other cases, the person might actually be taking advantage of you to commit fraud.

There are many examples on police blotters of such uses of someone else's card to commit fraud, such as in cases where someone is taking care of an elderly person or is managing someone's estate and fraudulently uses a card. But very often, in cases where you know the person committing the fraud, unless it is a blatant misuse of the card for an expensive transaction, it is more of a civil matter. You say you expected one thing; the person who used your card says he or she understood you to say another. Then it's up to an arbitration panel, jury, or judge to decide; such cases can be very expensive and time consuming, so they may not be worth pursuing.

Rather the best approach is to avoid this kind of situation by having a clearly written memo for less expensive purchases and a more extended agreement for more expensive purchases. Describe exactly what the person is to buy for you and the approximate amount to spend, along with a stated limit of the maximum amount. When the person returns with whatever they have bought, get a receipt. This way, you have clear proof of what you expected and what the other person should have understood. If the purchase or purchases far exceeded what you authorized, you have grounds to claim fraud to your credit card provider and perhaps even to the police. Usually, when you claim fraud and can show this—or the other party can't clearly show he or she didn't engage in fraud—you will prevail.

DEALING WITH UNAUTHORIZED CHARGES FROM A MERCHANT OR SERVICE PROVIDER

Another problem can occur when you give a merchant or service provider your card number for a particular product or service, but then that person charges you more than you expected or agreed to. This can be handled in a number of ways, depending on the circumstances. What you don't want to do is put in a fraud claim for something that is a misunderstanding or a good faith error that you can resolve by talking to the seller.

Resolving a Misunderstanding or Miscommunication

Sometimes a genuine misunderstanding occurs, where the seller thought you wanted additional products, wanted to modify or customize something, or requested additional services. Or the problem might be due to the seller expecting you to pay an additional fee, while you thought there would be no charge. In this case, there is no fraud, just a miscommunication, and often these are resolved by splitting the difference—the seller refunds you half of the amount, or perhaps it might be handled by including additional products or services. If the amount is significant enough, however, it could be the basis for a civil suit to work out who is correct or what adjustment should be made—and often a credit card company will urge you to settle this kind of disagreement about what you expected and received and the charges.

Resolving Billing Errors

This also may not be a case of fraud if it is simply a mistake If you point it out to the seller, it can usually be corrected quickly. Some typical errors are charges that list the wrong date, the wrong amount listed for an item, or math errors resulting in an incorrect total; bills that were sent to the wrong address after you previously gave the seller your current address at least twenty days before the end of the billing period; charges where you want an explanation or written proof of purchase after you claim there might be an error; and duplicate charges for the same thing. In such cases, once you contact the seller, explain the situation, and discuss the problem; that is usually enough for the problem to be resolved. Any mistake on either side is corrected, and you get a refund or additional products or services if due.

Sometimes you can simply make a phone call, discuss the matter, and get it corrected, especially if the merchant or service provider is located near you. Or if this is a long-distance purchase or payment, write to the creditor at the address for billing inquiries if different from that for sending your payments, and include your name, address, account number, and description of the billing error. The FTC has an example of a letter you can use to do this. Just insert your information as indicated, and feel free to adapt the letter to put it in your own words:

[Your Name]
[Your Address]
[Your City, State, Zip Code]

[Your Account Number]
[Name of Creditor]
[Billing Inquiries]
[Address]
[City, State, Zip Code]

Dear °°°°°°:

I am writing to dispute a billing error in the amount of [$_____] on my account. The amount is inaccurate because [describe the problem]. I am requesting that the error be corrected, that any finance and other charges related to the disputed amount be credited as well, and that I receive an accurate statement.

Enclosed are copies of [use this sentence to describe any information you are enclosing, like sales slips or payment records] supporting my position. Please investigate this matter and correct the billing error as soon as possible.

Sincerely,
[Your name]

Enclosures: [List the enclosures]

You should send your letter to reach the seller within sixty days of when the first incorrect bill was sent to you, and the FTC recommends sending it by certified mail with a return receipt request so you can show what you sent to the seller. You should also include a copy (not an original) of the sales slips or other documents that support your position, and keep a copy of this letter, too.

The seller is supposed to acknowledge receiving your complaint letter within thirty days of receiving it, unless you have already resolved the problem. The seller should also resolve the dispute with you within two billing cycles and not more than ninety days after receiving your letter.

Often these kinds of errors are resolved as soon as you bring the mistake to the attention of the seller. Or if the resolution takes a while for an investigation, you can withhold any payment you haven't yet made for the transaction you are disputing. But if you are supposed to pay any part of the bill you don't question, including any finance charges on the undisputed amount, and you don't pay, then the seller could put the amount claimed into collection or if the bill is large enough, pursue this in small claims court. However, if you do question the charges, even if you have paid in the past by credit card and the seller still has your number, he or she should not put through any charges, even if these are regular payments that are not part of the amount that is disputed as an error. Should the seller do so, and you are later unable to resolve the initial issue, this unauthorized charge could be considered potential grounds for fraud.

In any case, while the seller is investigating your claim that there was an error in billing, he or she cannot take any legal or other action to collect the disputed amount and any related charges, including finance charges, according to the FTC. Also, your credit card company can't close or restrict your account, although it can apply the disputed amount against your credit limit.

During this investigation, the seller also can't threaten your credit rating, report you as delinquent, increase your debt, or close your account because you have disputed your bill, although the seller can report that you are challenging it. This also means that another seller can't deny you credit because you are disputing a bill with another seller.

If after investigating, the seller discovers the billing was in error, the seller has to explain to you in writing the corrections that will be made.

Additionally, besides crediting your credit or debit card account that amount, the seller has to remove all finance charges, late fees, or other charges related to the error.

Should the seller determine that you owe or owed a portion of the disputed amount, he or she must give you a written explanation, and you can request copies of documents that show you owe the money.

If the seller's investigation shows the bill was correct, he or she must tell you promptly and in writing how much you owe or why, and you can ask for copies of documents that show this. Then, once it is clear you owe the disputed amount, you will also be responsible for any finance charges that accumulated while you disputed the amount and the seller investigated. You may also have to pay the minimum amount previously due that you didn't pay because of the dispute.

Should you disagree with the investigation results, you can write to the seller within ten days of getting the seller's explanation that you owe the money. You can even say that you refuse to pay the amount in dispute. However, now the seller can begin collection procedures, such as turning your account over to a collection company as delinquent, along with a statement that you don't think you owe the money. The seller is supposed to tell you to whom he or she has given these reports—such as to Experian, Transworld, or Equifax. But if you then resolve the dispute with the seller, the seller has to quickly report any resolution to anyone who got the report of the debt.

What the seller can't do, however, is charge your card for what the creditor thinks is the amount owed plus any finance or late fee charges, even if the seller wins the dispute and has your card on file. You still have to approve the seller charging your card, though the seller can now report the debt as being owed.

In fact, there is a penalty for a seller who doesn't follow these settlement procedures, according to the FTC. As the FTC notes in an advisory on "Disputing Credit Card Charges,"

> Any creditor who fails to follow the settlement procedures may not collect the amount in dispute, or any related finance charges, up to $50, even if the bill turns out to be correct. For example, if a creditor acknowledges your complaint in 45 days—15 days too late—or takes more than two billing cycles to resolve a dispute, the penalty applies. The penalty also applies if a creditor threatens to report—or improperly reports—your failure to pay during the dispute period. [1]

In other words, you have various protections that come into play under the FCBA, although in practice, when you point out an error, the seller or service provider is likely to quickly take steps to correct it. And often sellers and service providers who have an established business, ties to the community, or several years of business will want to settle these issues promptly, because they are well aware of the potential damage to their reputation if word gets around about their errors and refusal to correct these problems quickly.

Dealing with Charges for Goods or Services You Didn't Accept Due to Poor Quality Problems

If you have a complaint that the quality of the goods or services was unacceptable or of less value than the advertised price, this is not the same as an error in billing. The same is true if you did not receive the goods in a timely manner as promised or if they arrived in a damaged condition. Normally, this is not a question of fraud if it is a onetime or rare error by the seller and if the seller agrees to make things right, such as by charging you less, replacing damaged goods, giving you a discount for a delayed delivery, or otherwise making amends. In fact, making such adjustment is good business sense for a company that values its reputation and has a long history of success in its industry.

On the other hand, if the company doesn't make things right, falsely blames you for any problems, or has a pattern of misrepresenting its goods or services to many other consumers, you have a couple of options, depending on the amount you paid on your credit or debit card. If you paid with a check or cash, your usual recourse is to take the matter to small claims court if it's worth the time and effort or chalk it up to a learning experience and forget about doing anything. But if you used a credit or debit card for a product or service you claim is below the expected and advertised quality, there are more options.

First, return the product with a letter explaining why it is unsatisfactory, or, similarly, write a letter describing why the service was unacceptable or even caused you damage. Ask the company to give you a refund. If you can't work out an agreement that is acceptable to you, complain to your credit or debit card company about the product or service. If the company agrees, it will commonly refund you the money.

In this case, where you are not claiming fraud, you wouldn't normally contact your bank.

In the event that both the seller and your credit or debit card company won't provide you with a refund, you might take the matter to small claims court if the amount is large enough—say at least $500 to $1,000, since it will cost about $50 to $100 to file a complaint and then you have to serve the papers to go to court. However, before filing, it makes sense to advise the seller and even your credit/debit card company that you plan to do this. Give them the opportunity to work out a settlement with you, rather than going to the expense of pursuing a suit. In fact, even if you don't plan to go to court in the end, a threat of a suit might be enough to get the seller or credit/debit card company to settle the case, after recognizing that you are very serious about pursuing the matter. In writing the letter, clearly state the circumstances of the purchase and why you feel a refund, reduction in the charges, or whatever you are seeking to resolve your complaint is in order.

If you think what the seller did was serious enough, you can claim you were defrauded, because you were misled by the company or service provider about the nature or value of the service. Moreover, if you are complaining of fraud, you can report your claim to the bank issuing the debit or credit card or to the card company itself, though it is best not to do both, since this is a duplicate claim. Generally, it's faster if you report it to your bank, since you will get back your money in a day or two, rather than in two or three weeks with a credit/debit company. If the merchant disputes the claim, however, the money may come out of your account, though if you prevail it will be returned. If you can find others who feel similarly disaffected by their own experience with the company, you can use that to support your claim of fraud. And if you can show a widespread pattern, such as shown by complaints to the Better Business Bureau or to consumer complaint websites, so much the better. It is best to only use the fraud complaint when you are reporting an egregious case, since the seller will have a chance to dispute your fraud claim. Usually, however, if you have a basis for claiming fraud, you will win, since the credit/debit card companies and banks tend to resolve these claims of fraud to the benefit of the consumer, unless the complaint seems more like a dispute about the quality of the product or service than actual fraudulent behavior.

Dealing with Unauthorized Charges from an Unknown Party

Sometimes you may find that one or more unauthorized charges has appeared on your card from a company name or individual you don't recognize. This could well be a fraudulent use of your card by a stranger who has gotten your card number in any number of ways, and you want to report this as soon as possible. However, before you call in the number for unauthorized charges, check with the account holder, since it could be a charge from a purchase you have made but you don't recognize the name. Sometimes the business name to charge the card is different from the name of the company you know in doing business together.

The number of the business is usually on your card statement. Call it, and if you find the business name is linked to a purchase you legitimately made, there is no fraud—though it is a good idea if a person you do business with does advise you that the charge will be appear under a certain name so that you readily recognize it.

The other way to check out a charge is to keep a record of all your charges and the amounts—either in an online or a personal notebook. Then you can check the charge you don't recognize on your statement with the charges in your notebook. If there is a match, again no fraud.

However, after you have checked, if you don't recognize and didn't authorize the charge, immediately contact your credit card issuer or, if a debit card, contact your bank and report this is a fraud. The credit card company or bank will immediately stop your card and arrange to issue you a new one. You will also get a full refund, usually within one to three weeks with a credit card company, within the next day or two if it is a debit card issued by your bank. Since this is a case of someone using your card number while you still have the card, you have no liability. If you don't have your card because it was lost or stolen, then your liability is up to $50 of anything charged on the card, assuming you report it in a timely manner as previously noted.

The credit card or bank's fraud department will then investigate to try to determine who is responsible for the fraud and how they got your information, though often it is difficult to find out, especially when dealing with a criminal who is smart in covering his or her tracks. The scammer could have gotten your card through any of the fraudulent methods described in this book, such as accessing your information when you gave your card to someone in person or finding it on line. Usually, this just gets recorded so investigators can later look for any patterns, such as if a fraud ring seems to be operating in an area because a lot of the people experiencing credit card fraud live in that neighborhood.

Should you later discover that you made an error in reporting, immediately call to correct and withdraw your claim so your credit card company or bank can stop any review and investigation and consider the case closed. Otherwise, you could potentially open yourself up to a charge of filing a false claim and there could be penalties for that, depending on the amount involved and the number of unauthorized charges claimed.

8

PHISHING AND OTHER ONLINE FRAUDS

Online frauds to steal credit card information take various forms, such as computer hacks to steal your password and find your credit card numbers on your computer and seemingly legitimate requests to enter your credit card information on a form. Sometimes what starts as an offline theft, such as a thief obtaining credit card information from your mailbox or a store employee stealing your information can turn into the use of that information online for making purchases or for identity theft. The original thief may use it or sell it to a fraud gang who will use it or resell it until the card is reported lost, stolen, or used for unauthorized purchases. Another approach is to send you an e-mail attachment to open or a link to connect to that puts spyware on your computer to find credit card, password, or other information. The goal is to get information to be used to buy products or appear to be you.

In short, there is a whole underground industry trading in credit card information, and apart from taking steps to protect your card and your personal information already described, you should be aware of the various ways that fraudsters can gain information about your credit card account online.

BEWARE OF PHISHING EXPEDITIONS

One of the most popular ways of getting your credit card and other information is through various forms of "phishing," which essentially involves making it appear the scammer is some legitimate company. The goal is to get you to respond to an e-mail message by opening an attachment or clicking a link to go to a website where either you enter information or the software picks up information from your computer, while you believe you are communicating with the real company. Today, these messages are commonly spread by electronic means, though sometimes you may get a phone call asking for information, purportedly from a real company or organization, from the IRS, your bank, or a retailer where you have recently bought something.

These schemes have become increasingly sophisticated, making it more and more difficult to avoid them. The best approach may be to recognize when you think you have been phished, and then take the usual steps to monitor your bank or credit card account for fraudulent activity, report the problem, and stop any cards that might have been compromised.

How Phishing Works

Phishing works by the fraudster masquerading as a company or organization you trust, commonly sending you an e-mail or instant message that invites you to respond or click on a link to a website. In some cases if you click on a link or open an attachment it may have malware that can access information from your computer. Or the link to a website or address to which you are directed will ask you to enter details about yourself, which can then be used to steal your identity or access your bank account or credit card.

These can often be very hard to detect because the URL of a website in a hyperlink might appear to be legitimate. Sometimes the real site URL will show up in the lower-right hand bottom of the page or when you move your mouse over the hyperlink of the company in the e-mail, and obviously, if it doesn't match the claimed company e-mail, it's an indication that this is a phishing scam. But phishing tools have become so sophisticated that the hyperlink will often appear to show the URL of the real company even though the hyperlink will redirect you to the fraudster's link.

In some cases, the phishing software will capture your personal information, including your passwords, usernames, security codes, and credit card numbers, directly from your own computer; in other cases, you will be asked to enter the information, and because you trust the site and the message you have gotten about why your information is needed, you will enter it. It is as if you have given the fraudster a key to your front door. Then, when you aren't home, the fraudster can enter your house to take what he or she wants. The phisher is able to get this information by taking advantage of your trust, since you can't tell that the site you are visiting or the program is not real.

The types of legitimate companies and organizations spoofed in these messages run the gamut, though commonly they are banks, major retailers such as Amazon, and government agencies, such as the IRS or FBI. While these messages can be directed to private individuals, sometimes they are directed to employees, managers, and business owners, enabling the fraudsters to gain access to a database with names and personal information of thousands or millions of people. For instance, in 2011, fraudsters gained access to the credit card records of 110 million customers as a result of phishing a subcontractor account to access the system. In 2014, fraudsters were able to obtain the personal and credit card information for over 100 million shoppers at all 2,200 Home Depot stores by hacking into the Home Depot websites.

Some examples of the messages you might get:

- Your bank has detected some fraudulent activity and needs to check the security of your account, so please enter your name and password;
- The IRS has detected some problems with your filing, so it needs you to go to their website and enter your personal information to check this;
- There is a problem with your e-mail account, so you have to go there to change your password for security; and
- You owe a debt to the IRS, and you need to make arrangements to pay it now using your credit card.

The reasons for needing your information become more and more creative, as does the technology for accessing your computer and spoofing the websites of targeted companies to look real.

While phishing often involves broad attacks on millions of users, a more directed attack, called "spear phishing," targets specific individuals or companies. In this case, the fraudsters may gather personal information about a target to increase their probability of success, making the target think it must be real, since the e-mailer already has so much information. As a result, this technique has become the most successful; about 90 percent of all attacks use this approach.

Still another approach is called "cloned phishing," whereby the scammer takes a legitimate and previously delivered e-mail and uses its content and recipient addresses to create an almost identical or cloned e-mail. The fraudster then replaces the attachment or link in the e-mail with its own malicious version and it spoofs the e-mail address so the cloned e-mail appears to come from the original sender. Sometimes the fraudster claims this is a resend or updated version of the original.

Additionally, some fraudsters use what is called "whaling," in which a phishing e-mail is directed at senior executives, HR managers, or other high-placed targets in a business. Often this e-mail is crafted to appear like an important business e-mail sent from a legitimate business authority, such as a legal subpoena from a court or the FBI, a customer complaint, or a communication from another executive in the company. Sometimes the e-mail may ask the recipient to click a link to install special software to view the legal document.

For example, in one phishing scam costing companies millions, the scammers posed as company executives asking finance department employees to send wire transfers to pay for nonexistent goods or services. Sometimes they will send a PDF with the fake payment transfer instructions; in other cases, the employee is supposed to click on a link and then the fraudster will forward the payment details. In one variation, the fraudsters spoof the "from" address to make it seem like the e-mail is coming from a company executive along with instructions about sending out the payment to the indicated recipient now.[1]

In March 2016, many payroll and human resources professionals received fraudulent e-mails that appeared to come from their CEO requesting personnel details about employees. In this scheme, the professionals were asked to send W-2 forms with Social Security numbers and other personally identifiable information, and by the time the IRS sent out a warning about this, the fraudsters had already snared several payroll and human resources officers who mistakenly sent out data about thousands of employees.[2]

Other Types of Phishing

Still other types of phishing include these:

- You may get a message in an e-mail from a person claiming to be from the bank who gives you a phone number to call because of problems with your bank account. Once you call, you will get a message from a Voice-over-IP (VoIP) service (which allows phone calls to go digitally over the Internet) instructing you to enter your account number and PIN number. To convince you that the e-mail really is from a representative of your bank, the sending address may appear to have the domain name of your bank, thanks to the technical ability to spoof this. Or a VoIP service may use "vishing," or voice phishing, that will show a fake caller ID as your bank or another trusted organization.
- A fraudster's e-mail or link on a website might forward a consumer to the bank's legitimate website, but then place a pop-up window on the top of the page asking for your personal information. You think the bank is asking for it, but it goes right to the scammer.
- The fraudster uses tabnapping to hijack one of the tabs you use in browsing the Internet. Using this approach, the fraudster simply loads his or her fake pages into one of your open tabs, rather than directly take you to the fake site.
- In the "evil twins" phishing technique, the fraudster creates a fake wireless network that looks similar to a legitimate public network, such as you might find in hotels, coffee shops, and airports. Once someone logs onto this fake network, the fraudster tries to obtain the person's password and/or credit card information.

Another common approach by fraudsters is to use some type of technical deception to make a link in an e-mail and the spoofed website it appears to belong to the organization the fraudsters have spoofed. Sometimes they will use misspelled URLs or subdomains to trick individuals into thinking they are going to the real website. While many Web browsers will show you where the link actually goes if you hover your mouse over the link, sometimes the scammer can override this function. Then, when individuals go to the spoofed link, they may find the website looks real, so they put in their personal and financial information. In fact, some of these phony websites can look so real, from the Web address to the security certificates, that unless you have special knowledge, you are likely to be fooled. Moreover, sometimes a fraudster may get you to the spoofed page by using a covert redirect, in which the site is corrupted with a malicious pop-up dialogue box. You fill it in and, voila, the information you think you are sending to the website goes right to the scammer. For example, say you are using Facebook on your computer or mobile device. You may see a pop-up window asking if you would like to authorize an app, for example, to see a video, image, or file. If you authorize the app, the fraudster will receive a token, and your personal information could be sent along with it, which might include your e-mail address, birth date, contacts, and work history, and if the token permits your device to share even more information, the fraudster could obtain access to your mailbox, online presence, and friends list. Moreover, this app might even give the scammer the ability to control and operate your user account. Even if you don't authorize the app, you might still get redirected to the fraudster's website.

The social networking sites have become an especially prime target, since users are already involved in sharing a great deal of information. In fact, in experiments, researchers have found a success rate of over 70 percent for phishing attacks on social networks, meaning that 70 percent of the individuals receiving these attacks go to the link for more information.[3] So it becomes easy to post bogus links for users to click on for more information on a particular topic or offer a free PDF of a report or book that includes malware to access information from the user's computer. Or perhaps the offer seems compelling enough that the individual gives up not only an e-mail address but other personal information. Even a survey format might be used for getting information. While most of these reports and surveys may be provided for legitimate purposes, some are not.

In short, fraudsters use all kinds of phishing techniques, and they are continually evolving new technologies to access your information or new ploys to get you to share your information.

The Extent and Costs of the Phishing Scams

Phishing scams are widespread, causing not only individuals but companies billions of dollars through billions of attacks. For example, a January 2015 report from Symantec, one of the major Internet security companies, illustrates the extent of this fraud.[4] There were on average 30 to 50 spear phishing attacks per day over the year, and in several months, about 85 attacks per day; one month experienced 140 attacks; and primarily these attacks targeted organizations with 100–250 employees, accounting for about a third of the attacks. The major industries targeted were finance, insurance, and real estate, accounting for about 29 percent of the attacks, followed by manufacturing, about 21 percent of the attacks. The main type of data sought was real names (67 percent), home address, and government ID numbers, such as Social Security numbers (43 percent each). The other major types of information sought were financial information, birth dates, e-mail addresses, medical records, phone numbers, and user names and passwords (about 20–35 percent each). On average, 1 out of every 200 e-mails contained a virus, and about 5 percent of all e-mails contained a malicious URL. Even if a fraudster just gets your bank username and password, that can not only be the basis of a financial scam but also lead to identity theft.

Another report, by Phishing.Org, indicates that over half of Internet users get at least one phishing e-mail per day and over 100 billion spam e-mails are sent each day.[5] And according to the *Security Ledger*, the average cost for a business to recover from a successful phishing attack is $300,000, while the annual cost to deal with and fix a malicious software infection is $1.9 million.[6]

For individuals and companies combined, the losses due to phishing are in the billions of dollars, though the exact numbers vary from report to report. It is often hard to pinpoint these damages because they can include initial damages due to purchases made on credit card numbers; money stripped from bank accounts; and crimes committed in the name of an identity theft victim, resulting in lost employment, lost wages, legal expenses fighting criminal charges, law suits resulting from the actions of an identity thief, and more. So it is important to do all you can as an individual or as a business owner or manager to protect personal and financial information from being compromised by such a scam.

Protecting Yourself from Phishing

The messages and methods of phishing scams keep changing, so it's important to stay on top of the latest news about phishing, as well as alert others if you think someone has approached you about a phishing scam. More specifically, some of the suggestions for avoiding these scams are these, according to Phishing.org:[7]

- *Stay informed about phishing techniques.* You need to find out about new phishing scams as soon as possible. Follow the latest news reports, since new phishing techniques are continually being developed.
- *Keep the number of links you click to a minimum.* If the link comes from a trusted site, that's fine. But be aware that phishers mimic such sites and typically want additional information not normally requested by the site, such as your Social Security or credit card information. However, the big danger is if you click on links in random e-mails and instant messages, since hyperlinks are commonly the way that Internet users are led to a phishing website. A good way to check before you click is to hover over the link with your mouse and see if the actual link is the same as the URL of the organization to which you expect to go. URLs that have been shortened, such as those beginning with a tinyurl.com or a bitly link, such as http://huff.to/1ZJQsa3, could well be a scam, since anyone can go to these URL-shortening sites without registering and put in any long URL they want to shorten. So, as a general rule, don't click on any hyperlinks or links in any e-mail, since it could direct you to a fraudulent website. Instead, type the URL directly into your browser or set a website you commonly go to as a "favorite" or use a "bookmark."
- *Install an anti-phishing toolbar on your browser.* You can add this to most popular Internet browsers. The toolbar will quickly check the site you are visiting to compare it to any known phishing sites. If there's a hit, the toolbar will alert you.
- *Install antivirus software and keep it up to date.* Some popular Internet protection software programs, such as Trend Micro, Symantec, and McAfee, will also provide alerts about whether a link is trusted, unknown, or a suspected security risk. These software programs will also guard you against the known workarounds and

loopholes that hackers have discovered. Be sure to keep your software current, since new scams are continually being developed, and the software will add these new definitions as they are discovered.

- *Verify if a site is really secure.* If you are asked to provide any sensitive financial information online, make sure you really are on a secure website. If you are, it's fine to provide that information, such as to a health care provider, insurance company, or government agency. But before you enter sensitive information, check that the site's URL begins with "https." You should also see a closed lock icon near the address bar, and you might check for the site's security certificate, too.

- *Monitor your online accounts regularly.* Since hacking is always a possibility, check in with your online accounts to see that they appear the same as before. It helps to regularly change your passwords, too. This can get confusing if you have multiple accounts with a number of different passwords, but you might create a list or Excel file with the names of your accounts and the passwords, and then keep this in a very secure place. Also, create a longer password, with a mix of numbers and letters, upper- and lowercase, and some symbols such as % or #.

- *Check your bank accounts regularly.* Apart from checking other accounts, ideally check your bank account online every day or two to look for any irregularities. Report them immediately, and put in a fraud claim if warranted.

- *Keep your browser current.* To do so, accept the updates you may get from time to time, and download and install them. The reason for keeping your browser updated is that the popular browsers release security patches on a regular basis whenever they discover that phishers and other hackers have discovered a security hole. The patches are designed to plug these holes. Should you ignore the latest updates, you will make yourself more vulnerable to being targeted by a scam artist.

- *Use firewalls to keep out hackers, phishers, and other intruders.* The firewalls create one more buffer between your computer and individuals who are trying to get your information. One type of firewall is a type of software you install on your desktop; the other is a type of hardware. Using them together further increases your chances of avoiding the hackers, phishers, and other individuals who are trying to pry into your computer.

- *Be careful about pop-up windows.* These may appear on your computer, tablet, or smart phone when you visit a certain website or view an online ad. Sometimes these pop-ups are designed to get you to click on a link to go to a phishing site. You can block pop-ups on many popular browsing sites and choose to allow a particular pop-up. But even if you do this, an occasional pop-up might still slip through. In this case, don't click the "cancel" button, which could lead to a phishing site; instead click the "x" in the upper-right corner to stop the ad.
- *Avoid giving out your personal information over the Internet.* Be cautious when anyone on the Internet asks you for personal information. If you aren't sure if the company site is legit or the person requesting information is for real, go to the company's main website, get their phone number, and call them to see if the request for information is legit or if you can give the same information by phone.

Some other tips to protect against phishing are these:

- *Recognize the characteristics of suspected phishing e-mails.* These can initially seem legit, since they use the name and duplicate the image of a real company; they may also use the name of an actual employee at the company. However, in contrast to the more typical correspondence a company may send out, such as a monthly bill where you have a few weeks to pay, the e-mail may offer a promotional gift or the loss of a current account unless you respond quickly.
- *Be suspicious of any requests for personal information in an e-mail.* Sometimes these e-mails may appear to come from your bank, Facebook, PayPal, eBay, or other established company asking for you to verify your password or personal information. Never respond to these questions, and if in doubt, call your bank or other financial institution directly.
- *Look for any errors in a message.* Mistakes in English are often a sign of a scam, since many scammers are poorly educated or in

another country where English is a second language. Mistakes in spelling and grammar in a message to you are a sign to beware.

ALERT OTHERS ABOUT SCAMS YOU ENCOUNTER

If you do encounter a suspected scam or become a victim of one, spread the word. Besides alerting friends and associates so they can avoid being scammed, alert others who might spread the word as well. For instance, report any contact that might be a scam, whether via e-mail or phone, to the heads of organizations so they can alert their members and post this on your social media accounts.

An example of how this works is a message sent out by the Oakland Chamber of Commerce to its members and former members after some members of the local business communities in Oakland and neighboring Berkeley had reported being contacted by reps of a company claiming to be Chamber members and connected to the Chamber leadership. They were seeking to sell memberships and a wide range of services, including text marketing and credit card payment solutions, after which they asked for credit card information over the phone to set up new accounts. The Chamber e-mailed concluded: "It is unclear how they are using the data. [The company] and its representatives are not affiliated with the Oakland Chamber of Commerce and we have not endorsed any of their products or services."

There are also some websites where you can report your experiences and suspicions to be further investigated. Two, as described by Phishing.org, are:

- The U.S. government-operated website at http://www.us-cert.gov/nav/report_phishing.html provides information on where to send a copy of the e-mail or the website URL so experts can examine it. The government website also includes links with details on phishing scams and how to recognize them and protect yourself.
- The Anti-Phishing Working Group (APWG) (http://antiphishing.org/report-phishing) is another site for reporting phishing scams. It features a text box where you can copy and paste the contents of the suspicious e-mail you received, including the header and body

of the message. The sidebar of the website includes additional links of information to learn about phishing scams.

In short, be alert, be very alert so that you don't get scammed and so you can help others avoid being scammed, too.

SOME RECENT ONLINE SCAMS

Two recent credit card scams to get credit card information and/or money are the ransom scam and the bogus boss scam. These can take varying forms, depending on who is behind it, the amount of money that might be obtained, the amount of data at risk, and other factors. The specifics on online scams are continually evolving, so as people become alert about one scam and law enforcement goes after the perpetrators, the scammers are on to the next. Also making any kind of criminal or legal crackdown difficult is that the scammers are often based in another country, move around a lot, deal in untraceable funds, and are sophisticated in using computer hardware and software, so they are knowledgeable, agile, and elusive. Thus, the best protection is to stay up on the latest Internet and phone scams so you don't fall for the bait, such as by clicking the wrong link or opening up an infected file.

Ransomware

Ransomware is a kind of malware that can infect your computer; it locks or restricts the system or encrypts your files so you can't access them until you pay the "ransom" to regain access to the system or get an encryption key or unlock code. While the goal is normally to get a payment from the victim to get the ransomware to be removed, this doesn't always occur. Commonly the victim pays in the expectation of gaining access again, and the attacker requires the payment to be made in some convenient untraceable form, such as using a wire transfer, online payment voucher service, or Bitcoin.[8] Yet, even though these schemes generally just seek money, the scheme can be combined with obtaining personal and financial information that can be used for identity theft or credit card fraud. After all, in a successful ransomware scheme, the crooks already have access to your computer, so they can readily burrow deep to find this information.

According to an alert issued by the Department of Homeland Security's US-CERT program (which stands for United States Computer Emergency Response Team), the ransom from victims varies greatly, but is frequently $200–$400, payable in a virtual or untraceable currency.[9]

You can end up with ransomware on your computer in various ways. Often it comes through a phishing e-mail that you think is from a reliable source but contains malicious attachments. Or it may be as a result of what is called "drive-by downloading." Such downloading occurs when you unknowingly visit an infected website and the malware is downloaded and installed without your knowledge, a little like going through a drive-in and picking up an order, only to find you have been poisoned. Some ransomware is also spread through social media, such as when you use an instant messaging application. Also, some Web servers have been used to gain access into an organization's network.

The attack is so effective because it sends a scary message that can lead a victim to panic, so they click on a link or pay a ransom. For example, as the US-CERT alert notes, some typical intimidating messages are:

- "Your computer has been infected with a virus. Click here to resolve the issue."
- "Your computer was used to visit websites with illegal content. To unlock your computer, you must pay a $100 fine."
- "All files on your computer have been encrypted. You must pay this ransom within 72 hours to regain access to your data."[10]

For someone who depends on their computer for their daily work, such a message can be truly frightening, and the result is that many victims quickly pay. For instance, in 2012, Symantec, using data from 5,700 computers on a single server, found that nearly 3 percent of the users with infected computers paid the ransom, so whoever sent the virus averaged a profit of about $33,600 a day or $394,400 per month from a single server, meaning the cybercriminals are raking in multimillions or billions a year. In 2013, McAfee collected over 250,000 unique samples of ransomware, more than double what it obtained in the first quarter of 2012. And the threat has been growing with even more variants. Often when a system is infected with ransomware it becomes infected with other types of malware, including that which is designed to steal banking and other financial information. For example, before it was taken down by authorities, CryptoLocker infected computers with Upatre, which then downloaded GameOverZeus, a variant of the Zeus Tragan that steals banking and other types of data. Plus Upatre downloads CryptoLocker, which encrypts files on the infected system and asks for ransom. In other words, not just one malicious program but several programs are downloaded at the same time once your computer is infected.

There are all sorts of negative consequences if you become a victim, including the temporary or permanent loss of your sensitive or private information, a disruption of your everyday operations, and the financial costs of restoring your system and files. And even if you pay the ransom there is no guarantee the encrypted files will be released. The only guarantee is that the bad actors will get your money, and in some cases your banking information. Even after you decrypt the files, this doesn't mean you have removed the malware. It could lie dormant, ready to strike again sometime.[11]

Unfortunately, this malware can connect itself to any popular platform. For example, the malware known as Petya used the popular cloud storage service Dropbox as its carrier to force users to pay over $400 to regain access to their computers. The way it works is that victims would receive an e-mail designed to look like a professional looking for work and containing a Dropbox link that would supposedly enable the recipient to download and view the person's resume. But once the recipient does so, the file downloaded installs a Trojan that blocks any active security software and then downloads the Petya ransomware. First Petya overwrites the master boot record of the infected system, so you see a blank blue screen. Once you try to reboot your computer, you'll see a bright red screen with an ASCII skull and crossbones, and you can't even escape this by rebooting in safe mode, since Petya has already disabled your safe mode. Then, Petya advises the victim that the system has been locked with a "military-grade encryption algorithm," so the only way to regain access is to go to the dark web and pay for an encryption key with a Bitcoin worth $431, and if you don't pay within a certain time frame, the cost of getting this key is double that.[12]

So what can you do to protect yourself against such an attack, which can not only take your money but your personal and financial information. The US-CERT report[13] suggests these preventive measures to protect yourself from being affected:

- Have a data backup and recovery system in place for all critical information, and regularly test it to reduce the impact of data or system loss and to speed the recovery process. Ideally, keep this data on a separate device and store your backups offline. Plus, if you keep all of your credit card information in one place, you can quickly retrieve it so you can cancel and change all your cards.
- Use application whitelisting to help prevent malicious software and unapproved programs from running.
- Download the latest patches to keep your operating system and software up to date, since vulnerable applications and operating systems are the target of most attacks. This will reduce the number of entry points an attacker can use to get into your computer.
- Keep your antivirus software up to date, and scan all of the software you download from the Internet, before you execute it.
- Restrict the ability of others to install and run software applications on your computer, and limit the privileges you grant to others to install and run programs.
- Avoid enabling macros when you download any e-mail attachments, since if you enable macros, this will enable any embedded code to execute the malware on your computer. It is best for organizations to block e-mail messages with attachments if unsure of the source.
- Don't follow unsolicited Web links in e-mails. Often following these links is fine, but they can also lead you to websites with malicious software.

Even if a link or attachment seems to come from a trusted source, remember the problem of phishing. It may really be a trusted source, or may not. So look for information in the e-mail that will indicate that it really is coming from someone who knows you or has been in a conversation with you, such as a specific header referencing a prior communication or project you are working on together. Suspect generic e-mails with a general header, such as "How Are You Today?" "I have some helpful information for your project," or "I saw this article in the news and thought of you." If it comes with an attachment or link, e-mail the person at the address you know to be correct and ask if he or she did, in fact, send the e-mail. If not it could send in some malware as well as software that collects your personal and financial information.

The Bogus Boss Scam

Another scam to beware of is the bogus boss e-mail scam that can lead someone to give up private and financial data, as well as send money, thinking the boss has asked for it. Company owners have discovered that hundreds of thousands of dollars have been siphoned out of company accounts, while employees have unknowingly gone along with requests that facilitate this scam. And it is worldwide, targeting companies of all sizes.

For example, one target was a medium-sized company near Paris with fifty employees that had been making industrial equipment for over seventy-five years.[14] One day, while the owner was on a trip, someone called the accountant to say that an e-mail from the president with instructions on conducting a confidential transaction would be coming. Shortly thereafter, the accountant received an e-mail with the address of her boss indicating that the company was buying a company in Cyprus. Further, the e-mail said that the accountant would get a phone call from a consultant working with a lawyer who would give her instructions on how to transfer the money. The scammers also asked the accountant to act quickly, which is common in these schemes, so she wouldn't think about how this was an unusual request. Within two hours, she authorized a wire transfer of about $550,000. Fortunately, the bank held up three of the wire transfers, though one for about $110,000 went through. The bank was later held responsible for letting such a large amount through, but is appealing the judgment and seeking to put the blame on the company that asked for the transfer.

In any case, be suspicious if you receive a request as an employee or company owner to quickly send money anywhere. Some typical requests are:

- Someone claiming to be the boss of a company you work for asks the staff to make a wire transfer into a designated account (which will belong to the fraudster).
- Someone claims to be with the IT department of a bank saying they want to make a test transfer of funds—but it turns out this isn't really a test.
- Someone claims to be a supplier and asks that outstanding invoices be paid into a new bank account.
- An e-mail to employees has malware with links that authorize many small payments to the scammer's account.

While these examples are requests to transfer money, the same kind of approach can be used to commit credit card fraud or identity theft by asking an employee or company owner to provide personal or credit card information on customers. For instance, they might claim to be the new IT or security company that is testing the company's data system in order to make it even more secure.

In short, be ever aware of new potential ways that scammers may seek to get personal or financial information or money from you. And if you are considering the offer but are questioning whether it is for real or not, check out the source of any e-mails or phone calls to you. In the event the people you query don't give you answers you feel comfortable with or are evasive in avoiding responding to you, that's a big warning sign that this could be a scam. Should you suspect a problem, don't act to send any money, click any links, or download any files until you have checked out the e-mail and are sure it is what it claims to be and from a trusted source.

9

WHAT TO DO IF YOU ARE A VICTIM OF CREDIT CARD FRAUD OR PERSONAL IDENTITY THEFT

Con artists don't only use your credit card information to charge you for phony purchases or make purchases using your card but also in personal identity scams. This chapter deals with what to do when you suspect your credit card information might be used in this way. Some of the steps covered include contacting the card issuer and reporting the fraud, contacting the credit reporting agencies, filing a police report, filing a report with the FTC, and changing passwords and logins for your accounts.

THE POTENTIAL DAMAGES OF CREDIT CARD FRAUD AND WHAT TO DO

The basic damage of a simple credit card fraud is that someone can use your card or card number without your permission and rack up charges as long as the card remains valid. As previously noted, this can occur under various scenarios.

You Lose or Misplace the Card or It Is Stolen

The fraudster obtains your card when you lose it or leave it somewhere or by stealing it. In this case, the fraudster only has your name or company name, number, expiration date, and Social Security number, so he or she can use it in various places that don't require your zip code or driver's license or, in the case of a debit card, your PIN number, meaning retail transactions in stores and online. But the financial loss, if any, and the hassle of getting a new card is as far as it goes.

In this case, report the loss or theft of your card to your credit card company or to your bank in the case of a debit card, checking to see if you just misplaced it or left it somewhere. If you think you might still find it or get it back, you can delay reporting it, but monitor the activity of the credit card or bank account online or by phone to make sure no one has used your card since it went missing. You don't have to worry about any charges if you report the card missing or stolen within two days. After that, as long as you report it within sixty days, your maximum charge is $50, and the credit card company will pick up the balance. If you delay reporting the lost or stolen card any longer, you become responsible for anything charged on the card.

When you report that you no longer have your card due to either a loss or theft, you will get a replacement card within a week or two—or even faster, if you cover faster shipping. Ideally, you should have other cards you can use while waiting for your new card. To protect yourself from losing all of the cards at the same time, keep at least one card at home so you can access it if needed. In the event you find a lost card after you have reported it lost or stolen, cut it up and discard it, because that number has now been destroyed.

Normally, a fraudster will start to use a lost or stolen card as soon as feasible, wanting to rack up purchases before it is reported. And often that's as far as this goes. However, in some cases, a credit card loss or theft can open the door to other difficulties. For example, sometimes the name on the credit card could lead to more information about the person, such as address, phone number, and social media accounts. If so, it could potentially lead to identity theft. This is unlikely, as identity theft usually results from information gained online or from a theft of mail from a mailbox. Still, even after you have reported your credit card or debit card missing, be alert for anything odd that happens over the next few days or weeks that might relate to any information gained from your name or company name on the card. If you have been active on social media or promoting your name or business online, there is more of a chance of a fraudster making the connection between your card, your name, and other information out there about you. You certainly don't want to stop promoting a business, but just be aware of the slight risk of identity theft involved.

Something Is Wrong with a Charge on Your Card

When you are overcharged, incorrectly charged for something you didn't want, or charged for something you didn't receive, or the product is damaged or not as advertised, the first step is to talk to the merchant or service provider to get it corrected. If you get a refund on the disputed amount, no harm, no fraud. The matter is resolved. However, if you still object to the charge, you can file a complaint with your credit card company, which will then go through the process of disputing it with the merchant or service provider's merchant service account company. Commonly, at this stage you will get the disputed amount back while your claim is processed, and the merchant or service provider will get to respond to your complaint. In effect, reps from the two banks come together to weigh the relative strengths of the claims. If you have more evidence supporting your side and you win, then you keep your money, but if the other side wins, you are charged after all. A similar process occurs when you pay through PayPal. PayPal will have your credit card on file as backup, so if you don't have the money in PayPal to pay the claim if you lose, PayPal will draw the money from your credit card or from your bank directly if you are using a debit card.

If you feel the merchant or service provider took advantage of you, such as by talking you into something you didn't need, falsely advertising something, or claiming something would do something it didn't do, you can claim fraud. This is a more serious charge, so be sure you really feel you are justified in making this claim, especially if the vendor or service provider is part of your local or business community. If you do feel justified, go for a fraud claim; as a customer, you will normally be given the benefit of the doubt, so the opposing party has to disprove your claim. At this point, the process is much like when you submit a complaint, since a rep from your credit card company or debit card company/bank will initially process your claim, and usually your card company will return your money within a few days to a week, while your bank may return it in the next day or two. The merchant or service provider typically has twenty-one days to respond. You may have to then provide further materials supporting your complaint, and the merchant/service provider may have a final opportunity to provide further supporting material. If you don't reply with the information requested, the claim will go against you and you will end up paying the disputed amount. If the merchant/service provider makes a good case that you owe the money, he or she will temporarily get back the money returned to you. Then, a rep from your credit card company or bank will argue on your behalf against a rep from the other party's merchant account provider based on the material you have both submitted. They will decide whether the merchant or service provider gets your money or you get it back. As long as you provide the information requested and can reasonably show that you did not get the product as promised or were charged without your permission, you will usually win. That's because these fraud claims are normally resolved to the consumer's benefit.

However, be aware when you do file a fraud claim that there could be repercussions down the road. If you have made this claim against someone in your business community, that person may later find a way to retaliate against you, such as by badmouthing you to others. So make a fraud claim cautiously, when the problem is really more of a consumer or business dispute.

Your Credit Card Is Charged as a Result of an Online Free-Trial, Special Discount, or Other Scam to Obtain Your Credit Card Information

In this case, there is no question that your card information was obtained as part of scam. There are multiple variations on this kind of scam, but if you get caught in such an offer and get the run-around when you try to return the product or cancel the agreement and get a refund, you are clearly the victim of a fraud.

The first step to take, once you realize the scam—usually within a few days of getting the product and trying to return it—is to report it to your credit card company or, if you used a debit card, to your bank. They will then begin the usual dispute process described above and put the money back into your account, within a week or two if a credit card company or within a day or two if it's a debit card or direct withdrawal from your bank. In this case, it is very unlikely for the merchant to respond at all. They are simply trying to get money from as many victims as they can, and they depend on victims feeling they are stuck with the product or agreement for at least a month or two while they attempt to cancel future shipments. Once you protest, they go away. They are after the low-hanging fruit, so to speak, and once you claim fraud, you become hard to reach, so you soon get back your money, and that's that.

However, the one exception—and this could be a big one—is if the company that has obtained your credit card information for this product scam also takes your information for an identity theft scam, either conducted by itself or by selling your information to another company that will use it. Therefore, carefully monitor your credit card and bank statements for any odd transactions and take the other steps described for dealing with an identity theft, as described in the next section.

OTHER WAYS TO REDUCE YOUR RISK OF CREDIT CARD FRAUD OR IDENTITY THEFT

Even if you haven't yet become a victim, some ways to reduce your risk of becoming one are the following:

First, opt out of the prescreened credit card, loan, and insurance offers that come to you in the mail, which commonly are sent to individuals with credit problems. You will get less junk mail and have less information in your mailbox that others might steal. To do so, go to OptOutPrescreen (https://www.optoutprescreen.com), which is the official Consumer Reporting Industry website to accept opt-ins or opt-outs for offers of credit or insurance. It's free to opt out, and you can opt out for five years or forever.

Next, put your phone numbers in the Do Not Call Registry (https://www.donotcall.gov) if they aren't already there. This should reduce unwanted telemarketing calls, including for credit, loan, and insurance offers, once your number has been listed for thirty-one days, though not all telemarketers adhere to the restrictions. This is also the site for submitting a complaint if someone calls you who shouldn't call. If someone calls you claiming to represent the Do Not Call Registry inviting you to sign up for the registry, that person is a scammer seeking personal information from you. Go to the website directly to enter your phone number and other information.

Reduce the amount of personal information about you available on the Internet by using an opt-out service to remove your information from the major public data brokers. For example, one of these services, SafeShepherd (http://www.safeshepherd.com), will proactively remove your personal data from the Internet and marketing databases. As their website states:

> When we find a company publicizing or selling your personal information, we submit an opt-out request on your behalf, which deletes your record. If a website doesn't allow us to automatically remove your information, we'll provide straightforward instructions for how to handle the exposure. . . . You'll receive real-time alerts whenever you're found in a private database, or exposed online . . . before anyone else does. You can rest easy knowing that Safe Shepherd has your back; our privacy experts are on-call, ready to help you.

They even have a guide that lists many different places your data might appear and how you can contact them to opt out. There's no charge for monitoring the sites with your information, but they charge about $14 a month to remove this information. You can opt out individually, but it will take you much more time to do so. If you sign up for such a service, you can probably cancel after a few months after they have opted you out of the various databases where you were listed, or if you are concerned about getting relisted, you can continue your subscription.

Finally, to keep invaders out of your computer, you can turn on encryption on your computer, which will require a password to get through. If you have Windows, use Bitlocker to do this; if you have a Mac, use FileVault.

DEALING WITH BEING AN IDENTITY THEFT VICTIM

If you become a victim of identity theft, you are potentially in far more serious difficulty than simply having your credit card used by the fraudsters or sold to others to use before you stop it. Commonly, identity theft is combined with credit card fraud. The fraudster uses information from obtaining your credit card or getting you to put in information along with your credit card for what you think is a bona fide purchase in order to build the false identity. By stealing your identity, the fraudster can create a new credit card under your name and rack up debts with it. These debts may even include major purchases, including buying a car or a home using your name and Social Security number. And the fraudster can go on to commit crimes in your name so that you end up having a criminal record you don't even know about until the police happen to stop you for a traffic violation or you call in to report a crime and they check your record. You may even find yourself in jail while trying to explain that the person they think you are isn't you.

This kind of problem has become more and more common, because identity theft has become the fastest-growing crime in the United States. In 2013, according to a *Forbes* article by Laura Shin, 13.1 million people became victims, an average of one victim created every two minutes. And the cost of cleanup averages $500 per person, on top of the many hours you have to spend to clean up your record.[1] A key reason this crime has become pervasive is the ease of getting people's personal information in the digital age, since it is so readily available online or obtainable through phishing, hacking into computers, or installing malicious software.

If you have a child, there is also a danger that your child could be a victim of identity theft even if he or she doesn't have a credit card yet. In fact, in a recent survey, one in ten children were ID victims.[2] The reason is that when a fraudster uses an adult's credit card, it takes a relatively short time for the victim to recognize what happened and stop it. However, with a child's ID, the criminal could have up to eighteen years of access to credit by pairing the child's Social Security number with a different birth date to set up what's called a "synthetic identity." Then, the fraudster can use this to get credit cards and spend money— all in your child's name. Should you find there is a credit report in your child's name, it's an indication that your child has become an identity theft victim, since a credit report should not exist until your child first applies for credit as an adult.

The Identity Theft Time Bomb

What makes the theft of identity so pernicious is that victims do not realize that their identity is being used to essentially create a new life for a fraudster because of several factors. Michael R. Meinert, a Walnut Creek, California, attorney who specializes in consumer law, describes the problem as being that the fraudsters could lie low for some time before using your information. So, while you might act to stop your own credit cards once you notice any suspicious use, the fraudster could be creating a new set of credit cards in your name and you don't suspect anything, since the fraudster also changed your address, e-mail, and phone number by using your Social Security number. With these new cards, the fraudster could start building up debts you don't know about in another town, state, or even outside the country. Later, when the fraudster doesn't pay for these charges, you could end up with accumulating debts you don't know about either. Eventually, as these debts remain unpaid, they get reported to a credit reporting agency such as Experian, TransUnion, or Equifax or, as often happens, get passed on to a collection agency. Then these debts can be sold and resold to still other collection agencies for pennies on the dollar, who then try to collect from you. It is at this point—once the debt goes on your credit report or collectors start calling you—that you may discover that your identity has been used in this way, and then you have to go through all of the steps to prove that you are you; that can be very time consuming and expensive.

A good first step is to report the identity theft to the police, which will help to document that you have been a victim and these debts have not been created by the real you. Then you have to proceed to write to all of the creditors and credit reporting agencies for each debt to show that you were a victim. You can also arrange for an attorney specializing in consumer law or a credit repair agency to do this for you. A lawyer may have more clout in writing to the creditors and collectors with cease and desist letters that advise them that you have been a victim and that they can't further contact you unless they wish to pursue the matter in court. Usually that will lead them to stop their collection efforts while you get your true identity back together. While you can still take these steps yourself by writing letters and providing documents to show that you are you and are not responsible for the actions taken in your name, these efforts can take a huge amount of time, and you may find the process draining and daunting. It can take up to two or three years, and sometimes even more.

Two Examples of Identity Theft Victims

The following stories illustrate the kind of havoc a stolen identity can create in someone's life.

Amy Krebs is the victim written about by Laura Shin in her article for *Forbes*. Amy got a call from a major credit card company in February 2013. The call was from the company's fraud department, saying that someone had tried to obtain a credit card using her name, address, and Social Security number. The caller wanted to know if she had signed up for a card. After she said she had not, the credit card rep said they had flagged the card and would deactivate it. Even so, the company sent the card to another person's address.

For the next two years Amy had to work on regaining her own identity. It was even more difficult because the identity thief had changed many of her passwords and security questions and answers. For example, when she went to Equifax, Experian, and TransUnion, she couldn't answer all of the four security questions, such as which of these four addresses have you lived at and which of these employers have you worked for. She couldn't get two of her reports, because the imposter had infiltrated her credit history and overrode Amy's security question responses. But eventually she got one of the reports by guessing questions. She discovered multiple accounts that weren't hers, plus multiple inquiries. And since she couldn't access her other two reports online, she had to order them by mail and include her birth certificate, Social Security card, and utility bills to prove she was who she claimed to be.

It turned out the imposter had been using her information for six months, and in that time, she had attempted to open up over fifty accounts in Amy's name. Even as Amy tried to correct things, the imposter kept opening up accounts in her name.

Among other things, she filed a police report and an FTC affidavit, which all victims have to do. She also placed a fraud alert on her credit reports and eventually froze them. Once she put the alert on her reports, she got multiple calls from credit card companies asking if she had tried to open up a credit account. She also found that some of the accounts had gone into collections, so they didn't show up on her credit report right away. One account was even listed with a medical collection agency, showing that the woman had used Amy's Social Security number to get medical attention. Plus she used Amy's identity to get accounts from utility and phone companies, so she had all she needed to set up an apartment. And then, of course, she never paid the electric, heat, or cable bills.

Eventually, the police did catch up with the imposter, since she had the cable turned on at her apartment, and she had goods and services mailed to her address. She even used her own name when she signed up for a utility or phone number. But since she linked that information to Amy's Social Security number, it included her fraudulent information, which is why Amy couldn't initially access her credit reports. All of her information, including a past employer she worked for, then came out, which made it easy for the police to find her. As part of her plea bargain, she didn't have to tell them where she got the information about Amy.

Initially, though, she didn't plead guilty, so Amy had to go through a series of court procedures, which began with a complaint in municipal court followed by a review by a grand jury, where she had to give testimony. After the grand jury indicted her, there was a pretrial and trial. At this point she did plead guilty, but it would seem she got off easy, considering all that Amy had to go through to get back her good name. Since she was charged with a nonviolent felony, she did not serve any jail time. She just did community service. This infuriated Amy, because, as she told Shin: "Identity theft is a revenue stream for criminals, and this outcome means it's much easier to be a criminal of identity theft than a criminal manufacturing drugs."[3]

The process of regaining her identity was particularly daunting for Amy, because she had to continually prove who she was to different companies that have different methods for getting prospective customers to prove they are who they say they are. Especially galling was that Amy had to prove who she was to a greater extent than the criminal getting the goods and services. "You're treated like you're trying to get out of paying for something," Amy said.

Another hurdle Amy encountered along the way to reclaiming her identity was getting collection agencies to remove her debt, which wasn't really hers, from their records. In one case, she had to deal with both the original company and the collection agency by sending all of her information showing that she had been an identity theft victim. But after the agency said the account would be taken off their books, six month later, a different collection agency called seeking the same balance plus interest. So she had to prove who she was and wasn't all over again because of the way collection agencies sell debts to other agencies as part of a package of debts to collect. Eventually, she had an attorney who was working with her on a pro bono basis send the company a cease and desist letter, after which the original company wrote to her to say the debt had been removed.

Besides the hassle of dealing with the debt collectors, she also had to collect all of her medical information to make sure it was her own, and if it was not, she couldn't do anything to challenge it because of current laws protecting medical records.

Needless to say, she found the whole process one that created all kinds of havoc in her life. As she reported: "It's the most time-consuming, upsetting, emotional event you have to go through. Somebody went in and so easily removed my information and had their information override mine on this all important, encompassing document—my credit report. . . . Some lunatic has barely any information about me and gets access to all these goods and services—yet I have to fill out all these affidavits and turn in my utility bills and all my personal data to remove this fraudulent charge. The companies didn't ask anywhere near that when they extended the credit. But now that it affects their bottom line, they turn around and make me do all this."[4]

Another identity theft victim had a somewhat easier time of it, since her thief only used her card to successfully open up accounts in four stores, where she racked up bills of about $6,000. What this victim, described in a *New York Times* article by Molly Wood, found so surprising is how easy it was for an identity thief to open up accounts online or possibly in person and immediately begin shopping, even before the store card is processed. For instance, in each case, the victim received the store card at her house seven to ten business days later.

Since each store's applications required a Social Security number to sign up, and some stores ask for a driver's license number, this means the thief has obtained this information or someone in the store processing these applications has not followed the proper procedures to make sure she was the one doing the shopping. To correct this information, this victim found a fraud protection service, ProtectMyID somewhat helpful, since the service assigned her a case manager, who set up a conference call where they called each company who had checked her credit or issued a card in her name, and then she explained she had been a victim of fraud. Initially, the case manager made the call while the victim was on hold and then put her on the conference call so she could verify her identity. However, some of the respondents at these stores were a little disorganized. One referred her to its small card-issuing bank, which had one fraud prevention agent who wasn't there at the time, requiring further follow up. Two other stores asked her to fill out a paper affidavit that she would receive in the next week or two, and she had to mail it back for them to clear the accounts from her name. Just one store had already recognized this was a fraudulent transaction and had shut down her card.

But the most useful action was filing an online police report, and then sending dispute letters with a copy of the report to each credit bureau. Since the protection agency she used was affiliated with Experian, she filed a dispute with them, and then they prepared a letter for her to send to Equifax and TransUnion listing all the creditors with which fraudulent accounts were opened. Though it normally takes thirty to sixty days to process a dispute, and inquiries remain on your credit records for that time, because she had a police report attached, Experian resolved the dispute in one day and immediately purged all offending accounts. The police report then resulted in an extended fraud alert in which the big three agencies monitored her credit for seven years, instead of the ninety days they usually do without a police report.

In the end, this victim was far luckier than the more common experience of identity thieves buying things before their ability to create credit accounts at stores is shut down. She also experienced the common problem that consumers encounter of being able to do little to protect themselves from identity theft when companies that offer credit do little to make sure that people seeking credit are really who they say they are. And then the police often don't do much to find the perpetrator and make an arrest. But at least their report is useful in cleaning up a stolen identity, and sometimes a credit-protection service can help. In fact, some stores may offer this service for free, such as this victim found in the course of cleaning up her credit record.

HOW TO AVOID BECOMING AN IDENTITY THEFT VICTIM

It may be impossible to avoid having your credit card and personal information hacked or stolen, especially when fraudsters are able to hack into and steal millions of credit card numbers along with personal information from store databases. Plus fraudsters have become especially wily in the many different types of scams they perpetrate to get you to provide your credit card and personal information or to access your computer to get it. Still, there are approaches you can use to reduce the chances of becoming a victim. According to a *Washington Post* article by Jonnelle Marte, there are seven things you can do:[5]

1. *Use a different password for each online or other shopping account.* This way, if someone finds your username and password for one site they won't be able to use that information to go shopping at another store. Some sites, such as Amazon, also use multifactor authentication, whereby users have to enter a code sent to their e-mail or phone number when they try to log in, and then they have to provide that code as well. You can also ask retailers to remember your own devices, such as your home computer or smart phone, but ask for a code if anyone tries to log on from a different device. This can make it harder for thieves to access your account and make purchases in your name.

2. *Use a credit card rather than a debit card if you can.* Although both are protected from fraud, if an ID thief uses your debit card, the money comes directly from your bank and that could interfere with your ability to pay everyday bills while you wait for any money to be refunded, whereas the credit card company can reverse the fraudulent use without any money coming from you.

3. *Use a chip card rather than a regular credit card.* Increasingly retailers have them, since this has become a requirement, and these are more secure, since they create a new code each time they are used. This is supposed to be safer than the magnetic strips on the regular cards, which send your credit card company the same information for each transaction. They are also harder to copy, such as with the skimmer devices put on gas pumps and at ATMs. All the new cards banks are sending out will be chip cards. Request one to replace each of your current cards.

4. *Use a mobile pay application.* These apps, such as ApplePay, let you use your cell phone to shop, so you don't have to use your credit card. Instead, you just tap your phone to send a unique code to the retailer for each purchase, which fraudsters can't use. You even have an added protection with ApplePay, since you have to scan in your fingerprints to make a purchase, and fraudsters certainly can't copy those.

5. *Monitor your transactions.* Just as you should check your online bank or credit card statements every day for other credit card problems, from overcharges to incorrect purchases, you should be on the lookout for any unauthorized purchases, especially if you are frequently using your credit cards. If you don't have time to do this regular monitoring, set up an alert to send a message to your phone or e-mail whenever your card is used. Call your credit card company to see how to set this up.

6. *Use one card for shopping; another for paying your regular bills.* This will limit the potential for damage to your credit or personal information if your card for shopping is lost or stolen. Also, you won't have to change all your payment settings, since only one card has been compromised, so you just have to cancel and change that.

7. *Beware of phishing scams.* As previously noted, these come with various inducements to get you to click links, open attachments, and visit websites that can plant malware, ransomware, or spyware on your computer. Then, if they don't extract your personal and financial information directly, they may tantalize you with a sales promotion to get you to put in your credit and other information yourself. During holidays such as Christmas, Valentine's Day, and Mother's Day, the phishers may appear to be legitimate retailers, especially by using logos that look like those of established retailers. So check any Web addresses included in the message, by putting your mouse over them and seeing if there is a match (if not, it could well be a phisher), and don't click any links. Rather, go directly to the retailer's website to find out more about the offer and put in any information to make an online purchase there.

WHAT TO DO IF YOU BECOME AN IDENTITY THEFT VICTIM

If you do become an ID theft victim for whatever reason, act quickly to reduce any damage resulting from the breach. The more quickly you act, either on your own or with the help of an attorney or credit card monitoring service, the better. Here are some things to do and the order to do them in, according to an article posted on the popular social media site Reddit.[6]

1. Immediately report any stolen credit cards or missing checks to the appropriate bank or credit card company. Doing so will limit your liability if the fraudster uses your card or sells it to another user; your cost may even be nothing if you make the report within two days. Just be sure to contact all of the credit card companies, retailers, and banks for all of your cards or outstanding checks.

2. Place security freezes on all of the major credit reporting agencies, which include Experian, Equifax, and TransUnion. Also, place a freeze with Innovis Security Freezes, which is another less well-known reporting service. By freezing your credit reports, you prevent any bank or lender from pulling your reports, which will prevent identity fraudsters from opening lines of credit, obtaining credit cards, or gaining other loans in your name. The downside of doing this is you won't be able to take out your own loans or credit lines unless you temporarily or permanently unfreeze your accounts. Once you do request a freeze, each reporting agency will send you a confirmation letter with a PIN code, which you have to use to unfreeze the account. Be sure to keep the PIN in a secure place so you can access it in the future—otherwise you could be permanently locked out of your own account, along with the fraudster.

3. For convenience, place a security freeze with ChexSystems, a service that is used by 80 percent of banks and credit units to screen new customers. This procedure works just like reporting any credit card or ID theft with the separate credit reporting companies, except it makes it harder for thieves to open a bank account in your name at most banks. Although many smaller banks don't participate in this ChexSystems program, the service

will pass on your information to the larger banks in its network. This freeze will also reduce the damages due to a common scam in which a thief opens a new account and makes a large cash withdrawal from an ATM, resulting in a negative balance and damaging your credit when the bank or credit union charges off the account—or a collection agency handling the account for the bank does this.

4. File an identity theft affidavit online with the FTC. Save a copy and print it. Also, get your affidavit notarized by going to a notary public. Typically the cost is $10 per signature, though some banks offer notary services for free. Wait until the notary tells you to sign, since the notary has to witness your signature.

5. File a police report at a local police department. When you do, bring with you your filled-out affidavit, a government-issued ID such as your driver's license, a proof of your address, and a copy of the FTC memo to law enforcement.

6. Keep your notarized theft affidavit and police report in a safe, secure place, since together they make up your Identity Theft Report. You can use them in the event of any disputes with creditors to show you were the victim of identity theft and did not incur the debts created by the con artist after you filed these documents stating that you were an identity theft victim.

7. Next make sure your online presence is secure going forward. If you haven't already done so, install an antivirus program on your computer (such as from Norton, McAfee, or Trend Micro). The program will check for any malware, spyware, or ransomware, and remove them. Some other recommended programs for removing malicious programs are Microsoft Security Essentials, Avira, Bitdefender, Avast, and ESET.

8. If your computer has been infected, immediately change any passwords for your accounts, including your financial, social media, and e-mail accounts.

Following are some additional steps to take over the next few days, also recommended by the Reddit blog.

Obtain a copy of your credit report from all three reporting agencies to look for any newly opened accounts that you didn't authorize. You can get copies of these reports for free at www.annualcreditreport.com

or through a credit monitoring service. Or if you are already a subscriber to a service like Experian (www.experian.com) for a monthly fee, a report for that bureau will be included. Once you see your reports, do the following:

- Dispute any fraudulent accounts with each credit-reporting agency and with the fraud department of the bank or lender opening up the account.
- Look for any recent credit inquiries you didn't trigger as a result of applying for a mortgage, car loan, or new store account. Such inquiries can be a sign of fraud.
- Check that any addresses on your credit report are actually your addresses, since fraudsters will open up accounts with their own addresses or change your address to one of theirs.
- Apart from disputing the fraudulent accounts, dispute any fraudulent addresses or inquiries on each of your credit bureau reports with that agency, as well as with the bank or lender's fraud department.

If all of this monitoring and disputing incorrect information on multiple accounts becomes daunting, you might hire a credit repair company to do this work for you. There are some national services such as Creditrepair.com, which has a starting package of $99.95 per month. There may be local services independently owned or affiliated with a national service as well. Just do a Web search on "credit repair" and your city and state or zip code to find companies near you.

Another thing to consider is signing up for a credit monitoring or protection service that provides you with a daily credit report for at least ninety days, and preferably a year. Some of these companies have been around for nearly a decade, such as LifeLock and Trusted ID, according to a *Wall Street Journal* article from 2008,[7] which shows that this has been a long-term problem, since the rise of social media. These companies combine both preventive and reactive approaches to preserving your identity and credit—most commonly by providing you with fraud alert and putting a freeze on your credit by contacting all of your accounts and the credit reporting agencies. The most popular services include TransUnion, Experian, Equifax, Fast3CreditScores, Privacy-Guard, FreeScoreOnline, IdentityProtect, True Credit, LifeLock, IdentityGuard, IdentityForce, IDShield (affiliated with Legal Shield), ProtectmyID, MetLifeDefender, TrustedId, IDWatchDog, and MyFico. The cost of these plans range from about $9 to $18 a month. You can find them listed and rated on some consumer sites, including www.consumeradvocate.org/id-theft-protection and http://www.top10creditreport.com/credit-monitoring-services. Aside from these paid services, you can also get a free report through CreditKarma (http://www.creditkarma.com). However, while these sites can alert you to breaches, you still have to write the letters to dispute the fraudulent accounts—or hire someone to write these for you.

In the event that you were affected by one of the large data breaches reported in the news, you may be able to get free credit monitoring for two or three years. Look for the website handling the breach, which you can usually find from the company's main site or do a Web search on the company name and "credit breach" to find it.

Regularly check your accounts—or check the reports from your credit monitoring service. You can also set up text alerts with your bank and credit card companies in case there are certain activities that are unusual and suspicious, such as an address change, multiple failed log-in attempts, and charges distant from your location. Continue to immediately dispute any fraudulent activity as soon as you discover it. If you receive any debt collection notices, dispute them within thirty days, which will protect your rights under the Fair Debt Collection Protection Act (FDCPA), and send any disputes via certified mail with a return receipt requested. This way, you document your efforts and can use this information if the debt collection agency begins to harass you.

If your tax information was stolen or if you think someone has filed or might try to file a fraudulent tax return in your name, notify the IRS. A fraudster may do this to get a refund. The form to file with the IRS is Form 14039, the Identity Theft Affidavit. After you fill it out, sign and mail it. Meanwhile, continue to file your taxes and pay any taxes due as usual. For further assistance, call the IRS Identity Protection Specialized Unit at 1-800-908-4490. You can also get more information on dealing with the IRS at http://www.irs.gov/irs-pdf/p5027.pdf.

Some additional tips to further protect yourself in the future are:

1. Change the passwords for all your important accounts, and use two-factor authentication (2FA) if you can, especially for your e-

mail accounts and your online banking. Most of the big banks like Wells Fargo and Bank of America already do this, as do Yahoo!, Facebook, and Twitter. A complete list of all of the companies that support this approach is listed at https://twofactorauth.org. The advantage of using the two factors is that it prevents anyone who happens to get your password from logging in because they have to put in a second backup code. But if you do this, make sure you print out or keep a record of these backup codes in a safe place, because if you lose them, you won't be able to get into your account either. Another approach is to use passwords that are too long to remember. Use a password manager such as 1Password or LastPass to securely store them or create your own record of them on an Excel file on a computer that isn't on the Internet so no one can hack into it.

2. Keep any important physical documents, such as your ID and sensitive documents, in a secure place, such as a fire-resistant safe deposit box or fireproof safe at home. Aside from your driver's license and cards you use regularly, only take these documents out as little as possible. As for your Social Security number, commit it to memory, and don't carry your Social Security card around with you.

3. When you dispose of documents with personal or financial information, shred them before you dispose of them, and preferably use a cross-cut or micro-cut shredder for the best protection from anyone trying to reassemble your documents. Though it is rare, anyone can look through your trash legally because any garbage container, if unlocked, is usually considered public property (though there are laws in some areas that prevent scavenging on the grounds that the trash is being given to the company that picks up your trash, so it legally belongs to them).

4. When you send any mail about your case, send it USPS certified mail, with return receipt requested, and keep a record of who you sent it to and what you sent, along with your certified mailing letter. This way you have a paper trail to document your case. Preferably, send copies, not originals, but if you do have to send an original, keep a copy of yourself. On the copy or a cover sheet, include the certified mail number, and when you get back the proof-of-receipt cards, attach them to your copies.

5. Keep good records of whatever you did in seeking to repair your credit and any other damages due to your identity theft. If legal, record any phone conversations, or, as appropriate, ask permission to record these conversations, and keep a copy of these conversations on your computer, SD card, or flash drive. You can make transcripts of these, too. You can use any number of inexpensive recording services such as Rev.com, which has an application for a smart phone where you just record, click save, and send it off to be transcribed; you get back the transcript in a few hours. The advantage of having these records is you can use them to document that you were a victim if you have any legal problems as a result of the credit card charges or crimes committed in your name.

6. Still another approach to protect yourself even before you become a victim is to place a fraud alert on your files with the three main credit bureaus. This way, any bank or credit agency will pause before approving credit requests in your name, though under the law, a creditor is only required to take reasonable precautions before extending credit. A fraudster might therefore still be able to overcome a challenge—and this could make it more time consuming for you to obtain credit yourself. Or for even more protection, whether you have been a victim or not, you can put a credit freeze on your credit bureau reports, which prevents any company from accessing your credit until you already have a business relationship with them, so your records are sealed from any new creditor. While you can contact the bureaus to unfreeze your records, this takes up to three days, and there may be a small fee each time you freeze and unfreeze your records, though the rules about credit freezes vary from state to state. In both cases, you can contact the credit bureaus yourself for an alert or a freeze, but a credit monitoring or identity-theft protection company can do it for you for their monthly service fee.

Part II

Protecting Yourself as a Merchant or Service Provider

10

PROTECTING YOURSELF FROM FRAUD BY CONSUMERS AND CLIENTS

As a merchant or service provider, you are similarly at risk from fraudsters who might gain information about you for credit card fraud and identity theft, just like any consumer, except that they might use your business credit card or company information. Thus, all of the cautions to protect yourself or advice on what to do if you become a victim as a consumer would apply to your business, too.

In addition, you have to be on the alert for consumers or clients who might seek to take advantage of you.

WHEN A PROBLEM IS A DISPUTE AND NOT A FRAUD

If a consumer or client has a legitimate dispute about not receiving a service, receiving poor service, or getting overcharged or otherwise feels wronged, then it is handled through the dispute process provided by your credit card company, bank, or PayPal, much like when you as a consumer have a complaint about service from another merchant or service provider. The only difference is that a complaint or dispute has been initiated against you.

Obviously, the best way to deal with such problems is to respond quickly when the consumer or client brings the problem to your attention. If you feel the person complaining is acting in good faith based on a problem of communication or misunderstanding, it is often a good idea to work out some kind of compromise where you offer to fix the problem, give the consumer a reduced price, or provide credit for a future purchase. In this way, you maintain a good relationship with your customer or client, and may not only avoid any credit card dispute, but also please the customer or client, resulting in future sales. It is also better to avoid such disputes because the consumer protection laws and customary retail practices give the benefit of the doubt to the consumer, so you are likely to lose.

However, if you are unable to resolve such a dispute or if a consumer or client files a complaint with their credit card company, bank, or PayPal, then be sure to respond by the deadlines provided. By doing so, you have the best chance of making your own case and prevailing if you can show certain evidence that tips the scales in your favor, such as a signed written contract with the consumer or client and a paper trail showing proof of delivery and e-mails from the client indicating satisfaction with your product or service. At this point, a rep from your respective credit providers will argue each side of the case and will determine whether the customer has a valid claim or you do, or if the claim might be settled by a partial refund by you.

As long as such a claim is only a single or rare occurrence, it shouldn't affect your merchant account. However, if you do have a trail of such complaints, especially if you lose any disputes, this could affect your merchant fees, resulting in higher charges for each sale, or it could make it harder to dispute subsequent claims, since you have a record of such disputes. In some cases, a merchant account provider might cancel your account and even look into whether you might be guilty of fraud yourself. Thus, you want to reduce the number of such disputes by settling them early where you can so disgruntled customers or clients don't resort to filing complaints against your business.

TYPES OF FRAUDS AGAINST MERCHANTS AND SERVICE PROVIDERS

This situation is quite different from when you do encounter a customer, client, or business service that actually attempts to defraud you under various circumstances. Some of these situations include the following:

1. A customer or client uses someone else's credit card, acquired by credit card fraud or identity theft.
2. A customer gives you a credit card after using a service that is declined and then makes excuses to avoid paying.
3. A customer or client seeks to obtain products or services for free by filing a fraud claim against you, based on a false claim, such as not receiving the product or service, not authorizing or participating in the transaction, asserting that the product or service was substandard, or returning a product after using it and seeking a refund.
4. A credit card processing service signs you up for an adhesion contract, which binds you to pay for the service even if the equipment doesn't work, you no longer want to use the service, or you go out of business—and you later find a huge number of complaints about that company.
5. A fraudster attempts to use your company name in a phishing scheme to get victims for a credit card fraud or identity theft.
6. A fraudster hacks into your database with information on your clients or customers.

The following chapters will describe how to protect yourself from credit card fraud, how to spot potential fraudsters, and what to do if you are a victim of different types of frauds.

11

ENCOURAGING CASH AND CASH-LIKE PAYMENTS

One simple way to avoid credit card fraud by customers and clients is to use cash-only payment arrangements. Apart from payments in cash, you can use money orders, cashier's checks, and direct bank deposits to reduce fraud.

SETTING UP A CASH ONLY SYSTEM

Requiring payments in cash only can work for certain kinds of businesses where you are getting small payments for merchandise or services. Or you can require cash for payments under a certain amount, such as $10, $20, or $25. This also has the advantage of not paying merchant fees on credit card or PayPal transactions.

For example, many restaurants and convenience shops require cash-only payments. So do entertainment venues: many movie theaters, small independent theaters, concert halls, and sporting events commonly ask for payments in cash, as do individuals doing workshops and seminars. Many meetings require cash payments, too.

You can also use a pay-in-advance ticketing service, such as Event-Brite (https://www.eventbrite.com) or WePay (https://go.wepay.com), which will take a small commission, but if the event goes forward and you don't offer a refund unless you cancel the event, everyone has paid. These are especially good services where you are having an event and you know people are committed to attend—or at least they are more likely to do so—because they have already paid, and you know you will get your money within a few days after the event. Certain platforms for events, such as Meetup, make arrangements with such services where people automatically pay when they sign up for the event, unless, usually for a larger fee, they opt to pay at the door, if that option is available. In some cases, you have to pay in advance to play.

The advantage of this cash-only system is that you don't have any risk of credit card fraud, and only rarely do those who pay in advance ask for their money back, which you can deal with on a case-by-case basis.

The one issue that sometimes comes up in these cash-only systems is that occasionally people don't have cash and want to pay by check or credit card. In that case, a credit card payment for a small sum is usually fine if the person gives you a card with a current expiration date and you can take the credit card information from the card for later processing. Also take the person's phone number and e-mail, preferably off a business card, so you can call if there is any problem with the card being declined. Usually, though, in such situations, the card will be fine. Usually, if there is a card decline, it will be just because the person has gone over the limit, and he or she will readily correct the problem with another card. Usually a check in this situation will be fine, too, especially because a person who gives you a bad check will risk a high return fee (about $35) versus your bad check charge (about $10).

In any event, whether to accept an alternative pay method is your call, though in most cases, the usual practice is for companies to accept credit cards for purchases of products when they have a way to process the card in advance, whereas service providers commonly accept either a credit card payment or a check before a program or before or after providing a service.

CREATING AN INCENTIVE FOR CASH PAYMENTS

Another approach is to get as many cash payments as you can to reduce the potential for credit card fraud by offering a discount for cash payments or for cash-like payments, such as a money order or cashier's check for larger purchases. You do have to be aware of the potential for a money order or cashier's check to be phony, but it is rare in local transactions. These are more likely where someone is making an e-mail purchase or in e-mail scams where you are asked to wire a refund from an overpayment. A direct deposit in a bank account might also be an approach you can use for local transactions, in transactions where your bank has a branch where the person is located, or even in online transactions. The danger here is you are giving the person your bank and bank account number. However, that might be fine where you have met the individual personally or, even better, have an ongoing relationship. Just be cautious in accepting these. If in doubt about the validity of the check or money order, check with your bank or with a branch of the bank on which the money order or cashier's check is drawn to see if it is valid. In the case of a really good forgery, you will only find out about two to three weeks later when the bank finishes processing the paperwork.

Many companies do offer this pay-by-cash incentive, where you pay less for using cash—commonly about 5–25 percent less—or think of it as paying more for using a credit card. Gas stations often have a reduced price for cash payments, commonly 5–10 cents less per gallon than payments by credit card. Alternatively, some companies charge a 5 percent fee for using a credit card in order to recoup their own charges in processing a card payment.

THE RISKS OF A CASH-ONLY SYSTEM

Only dealing in cash or cash-like payments can be great for reducing your potential for credit card fraud, but be aware that there are three other risks, two already mentioned, which is why many companies still prefer accepting credit cards and the potential for fraud that goes along with that.

1. The risk that a money order or cashier's check may be a phony, designed to get products or services for free, since it will take about two to three weeks for the bank to discover these instruments are phony.
2. The risk that a direct deposit will expose your account information to a fraudster who will later use that for taking money out of your bank or for identity theft.

3. The risk of a burglary or robbery once it is known that you accept
    cash-only transactions, since this approach suggests you have
    large amounts of cash on hand. A burglar might try to sneak in
    after hours to snare this cash—or an armed robber may appear in
    your place of business and demand you hand over the cash.

All of these risks are rare, so in the long run, getting as much payment in cash as you can is a good way to go. In general, the vast
majority, if not all customers, will make legitimate cash payments, and
you will be fine.

12

THE POTENTIAL FOR CREDIT CARD FRAUD

Generally, credit card fraud is conducted by individual clients seeking to get a product or service for free by using another person's credit card or making a false claim of fraud against you based on some reason they claim to their credit card company or PayPal. But sometimes you will face a customer or client who is actually part of a larger network that provides stolen cards, such as obtained from robberies, or credit card numbers from hacks. The use of stolen credit cards and numbers can be quite profitable. The typical victims here are usually retail stores or gas stations, where a fraudster can quickly make a purchase and leave. Sometimes these numbers are obtained through a ring of credit card fraudsters who get stolen numbers and manufacture cards, and sometimes a fraudster is on the inside of the targeted company and uses their employee status to make the purchases on the fraudulent cards. In fact, the extent of credit card fraud is so huge that according to the Nilson Report, fraud with credit, debit, and prepaid cards resulted in over $16 billion in losses around the world in 2014, with nearly $8 billion of that in the United States.[1]

For example, one couple in Brooklyn made about $100,000 in purchases using a number of credit cards they had purchased through an associate. As described in a March 1, 2016, article in the *New York Daily News*,[2] the police arrested twenty-two-year-old Michael Mena and his girlfriend, Maggie Ferreira, twenty-five, who had gone on a huge spending spree with stolen cards after employees at the Kings

Plaza Shopping Center got suspicious of the couple's behavior. They had obtained gift cards using American Express and Visa Cards, which they obtained through a male acquaintance who manufactured the cards using stolen customer information. The acquaintance gave the cards to Maggie, who then took them, some with over $10,000 in credit available, to her boyfriend, Mena, who worked at a kiosk in the shopping center. Mena turned them into gift cards and Maggie then returned them to the associate, who gave her a 10 percent cut, which she split with Mena. Or they used the gift cards themselves to make purchases.

They carried out their first series of scams on December 23, 2015, when they used a stolen American Express card sixteen times to buy $3,200 in gift cards. Then, on January 8, they stole more than $18,000 using another phony card. Finally, on January 9, thinking they were getting away with what seemed like the perfect scam, they used a third victim's card twenty-six times to purchase over $37,000 in gift cards. They even used this approach to spend over $50,000 on a Carnival cruise and a used car.

It seemed like a perfect scam, since once the gift cards were purchased, they were untraceable and could be used like cash. But authorities at the Kings Plaza Shopping Center became suspicious because of the high volume of transactions Mena processed with Maggie, and they called the police. They had little defense, since Mena was caught on video six times receiving the fraudulent credit cards from Maggie, and the police also had multiple signed receipts by her with different names on them.

In another case, two New Yorkers were charged as part of a credit card theft ring that operated in Ohio, New York, and Pennsylvania, using over twenty-five different credit card numbers, most associated with the Toronto Dominion Bank, to buy gift cards valued at more than $150,000 from stores in Northeast Ohio.[3] They also used gift cards to buy other merchandise from stores in New York and Pennsylvania, though they were initially charged for the Ohio crimes. Much like Mena and Maggie, the men obtained stolen credit card numbers that they used to buy gift cards at Giant Eagle and Get Go stores in three states and at least three communities in Northeast Ohio. At one store in this area, the Giant Eagle Supermarket, they made over $9,000 in purchases.

While the police arrested the two men, Rondon Bernard and Raymond Caballero of New York State, and charged them with wire fraud and identity theft, they weren't sure how the men acquired the stolen card numbers. However, it may be due to credit card skimmers on gas pumps, which can steal credit card data. In any case, after the men were indicted, they were charged in court with over twenty counts, including theft and identity fraud.

In still another case, a Miami couple, Patricia Perez-Gonzalez and Alberto Companioni, engaged in a $2 million credit card fraud and identity theft scheme in which they mainly targeted seniors. They worked with a network of coconspirators to use stolen information to get around the usual safeguards against fraud, such as chip-enabled credit cards. They used American Express credit cards with chip technology and opened over forty accounts using stolen personal information. Then they had the cards shipped to various locations around the United States, often vacant homes and properties, where the couple and their coconspirators intercepted the cards. The couple went on a shopping spree to purchase luxury items and vacations, and Perez-Gonzalez used the cards to buy wholesale merchandise that she resold on her retail-clothing website, "Le Fashion Wheels." When law enforcement finally caught up with them and investigators conducted a search of their many Miami addresses, they found "dozens of credit cards in victims' names . . . forged identification and licenses, a credit card encoder, blank credit cards, more than ten phones labeled in the victims' names and merchandise purchased with the fraudulent American Express cards, including a Rolex watch, racing bikes, ski gear, Chanel bags and other designer clothing and accessories."[4]

While such credit card fraud rings may account for much of the fraud using stolen information to buy gift cards, a much simpler type of credit card fraud is simply a crime of opportunity by a single individual. For example, one man charged about $300 in transactions on a card he found in a Walmart after the card owner lost it there. The card owner reported the card loss to the police, but almost immediately the suspect used it to make purchases. The police were able to obtain a photo of the suspect from a security cam in the complex, and they sought the public's help in identifying the man, putting out a call through the media asking for tips.[5]

Normally, if you suspect someone is using stolen credit cards, ask for identifying information, such as a driver's license. Then, if you can, let the person know there is a problem with the gift card so you can't complete the transaction. When the suspected scammer is out of sight, call the police. You don't want to directly confront the suspect, which could up the odds that someone could get hurt. Once the police are involved, they can investigate. Or if it seems like a touchy situation, ask for the usual ID information, such as a driver's license, put through the purchase, and note the name and number on the card. Then call the police. In either case, whether you have put through the purchase or not, call the police as soon as possible to report your belief that someone is trying to use a fraudulent credit card, and be ready to cooperate with the police in giving a statement and viewing any videos of the suspect making a purchase. If the police catch the suspect, they can use your information to bolster their case.

The best strategy is to try to avoid accepting a stolen credit card in the first place and to have in place some guidelines for processing credit cards and gift cards to reduce the number of stolen cards you take in, such as asking to see an ID. If the name on the ID and on the card don't match, don't accept it (barring safety concerns for yourself). Report any suspicious behavior to the local police and, if you are in a mall, the mall authority so they can alert other merchants. If you do process the cards, keep any records of the purchase and pay close attention to the buyer so you can recall details if the charge card later proves to be stolen.

You might also use a credit card fraud protection service as well as equipment to process the new chip cards, since your credit card company or the bank issuing the card will assume liability, whereas if you accept regular cards or accept online orders, you assume the liability for any fraudulent purchases. More about these procedures in chapter 14.

13

AVOIDING CHARGEBACK FRAUDS

You may get chargebacks for perfectly valid reasons, such as if the customer did not get the merchandise or received it too late, the customer found the merchandise or service did not meet the expectations of quality, or the product or service was not as advertised. In such cases, the best way to avoid a chargeback is to have an open-door policy so a customer can reach you or one of your reps to discuss the problem. If the customer's complaint is valid, try to correct the problem by offering a partial refund, fixing something that was broken, giving the customer a credit or discount on a future purchase, or otherwise negotiating an agreement satisfactory to the customer. If you have really done wrong by the customer, you want to do what you can to correct it, which will generally avoid the chargeback as well as create a better relationship with your customer and lead to subsequent sales and referrals.

Some other reasons for legitimate chargebacks may occur for technical reasons, such as an expired card authorization, insufficient funds in the person's account when the charge comes through, or a bank processing error. Another reason might be a clerical mistake, such as a duplicate billing, an incorrect amount, or a promised refund that was not issued.

But some chargebacks may be initiated by dishonest customers trying to get merchandise for free, avoid paying for a service, or get merchandise or service for a reduced rate. In these cases, the benefit of the doubt goes to the consumer, even when that consumer is lying, if you can't prove it, due to consumer protection laws. Therefore, you want to watch for the warning signs of an unscrupulous customer or client so you can avoid entering into the transaction in the first place. You also should keep documentation on each transaction so that you are better able to reverse a chargeback and keep it reversed.

AN EXAMPLE OF A CHARGEBACK SCHEME

A good example of a fraudulent chargeback scheme is what happened to my cowriter, which inspired this book, as she noted in the foreword. Gini had sold a book for a client through her e-query service, Publishers Agents and Films (www.publishersagentsandfilms.com), which sends out personalized e-mails to publishers and agents, who then respond directly to the client. Through this process, one client got interest from several dozen editors and agents who wanted to see a proposal, which she didn't have. Accordingly, her husband wrote a proposal for her, but it was very badly written, so Gini indicated that she could rewrite it as well as do some needed research on other books in her market. After getting a go-ahead, Gini completed the proposal, they sent it off, and several weeks later they sold the book to a publisher.

But when Gini tried to charge for the additional work, the charge was declined. The husband said a first priority would be getting her paid, but after making various excuses, the wife sent Gini an e-mail asking if she would take the balance in trade. Gini felt there was nothing to trade for and was surprised by the request, since this was outwardly a very successful book, so she turned the offer down. Later she received a letter from the wife asking for a copy of the billing, which Gini had previously sent, and after no further communication from them, she received a chargeback notice for the first payment from her credit card company. The husband was now claiming fraud because he hadn't authorized or participated in the transaction. Gini disputed the chargeback with about three hundred pages of e-mails plus copies of the manuscript she rewrote and the original, showing that she had successfully done the work and that the husband was involved in the transaction. Her own credit card company reversed the chargeback, but the husband lied again to his own credit card company, again claiming he hadn't authorized or participated in the transaction, and the chargeback reversal was reversed. So the couple never paid for the charge that was declined—a total of about $1,200—and used the proposal Gini wrote to sell the book, which is now on the market.

It was a lesson in how a customer or client can easily set up a chargeback scam, for both in-person and online charges, though there is a greater risk for a scam where no card is presented, since the customer or client can easily claim a lack of authorization and participation. For example, even with extensive e-mails the client can always claim he didn't send them or can otherwise claim he or she wasn't the one using the card and giving card information over the phone or the Internet.

But there are various ways you can protect yourself. In a situation where you do the work or send the product before you charge the customer, rather than working on a retainer or advance payment, there is always risk, although most customers are honest. But to reduce your risk, you can seek to get paid in advance or use an agreement form that the customer or client has to sign to authorize your work or shipment of the product. Then, he or she is less likely to attempt a fraudulent chargeback or to win by doing so. Following are more specific ways to avoid chargebacks and how to fight a chargeback case.

PROTECTING YOURSELF FROM FRAUDULENT CHARGEBACKS

A key way to protect yourself is to take proactive measures to reduce the chances that someone will attempt a fraudulent chargeback and increase your chances to win if you do have to dispute a claim.

For transactions where no credit card is presented, which are increasingly common due to phone, Internet, and e-mail orders, maintain a physical record of customers authorizing the charges. To this end, include the customer's credit card number and V-code, address, and zip code, which merchant terminals typically ask for in authorizing a transaction.

If you are doing work for a client over a period of time, advise the client by e-mail of your estimated fee before you put through a charge and get an approval. Alternatively, continually update the client with the hours if charging on an hourly basis or with work components you have completed. Check with the customer or client by phone or e-mail from time to time to make sure he or she has gotten your billing and approves.

Keep a copy of all your e-mails, sent and received. Documenting your correspondences is another way to discourage and defeat fraud claims, although it doesn't work perfectly, as Gini's case illustrates. As you never know what a client may question or claim as fraud in the future, you want to have this documentation to back up your side of the story, both with the client and with your merchant account provider or bank.

If you have a physical store or see clients face-to-face, you are in a better position to protect against chargebacks, since you can require the customer or client to give you a card to swipe. If you have a swipe-only checkout, that is almost perfect insulation from fraudulent chargebacks, as described in an article on "How Companies Can Protect Themselves against Chargeback."[1] You can further substantiate that the charge was authorized by imprinting the charge on the customer's receipt and asking the customer to sign an order form or receipt, which you can compare with the signature on the back of the customer's card. If the card isn't signed, ask the customer to give you an ID, such as a driver's license or other government-issued ID with a photograph. A customer with intentions of disputing the charge will often back away from making the purchase with all of these proactive protections.

Still another way to protect yourself from fraud is to obtain agreements and contracts from clients for your products and services, especially if you are providing professional or ongoing services or are selling customized or expensive goods. And don't only give the customer or client a copy; ask him or her to sign it, showing agreement to and understanding of the service you are providing or what product you are selling. This agreement should indicate what you are providing and what you expect to be paid and when. It might include a reference to your accepting payments by credit card. Have the customer or client sign to indicate approval, and include a space for the client to include initials for approving each page. Having such a standard agreement or contract will show how you regularly operate, and many customers and clients will appreciate your professionalism as well as see the agreement as a protection for them, since it specifies what they will be receiving from you. It may additionally include timelines of what you will deliver when. Then, as long as you deliver as promised, this documentation will help refute any chargeback claims. If there should be unexpected delays, such as extremely bad weather, then talk to your customer or client to work out an extended delivery date. A legitimate customer or client will normally appreciate your concern and ability to quickly get on any problem and make any necessary corrections.

If you are involved with retail or face-to-face transactions, switch over to a point-of-sale system that is EMV (Europay, Mastercard, and Visa) compliant. This is the worldwide card payment standard that uses an embedded chip that sends a onetime unique code to process the payment. This makes it more difficult to duplicate credit cards, so fraud is more difficult and the payment is more secure. This became the new standard in the United States in October 15, 2015, and except for gas pumps and ATMs, which have until 2017 to switch over, using or not using this standard in a transaction shifts the liability for fraudulent purchases. Before this standard, the credit card companies and banks who issued cards were generally responsible for fraudulent transactions when a card was presented, but now they will only assume liability if you use the new equipment. Otherwise, you may be liable for any fraudulent transactions under these conditions. According to an article in the *National Law Review*,[2] you may be liable if:

- You do not use a point of sale system that is EMV compliant when you process a fraudulent transaction (including those involving lost or stolen cards) using the magnetic strip on a chip-enabled card.
- You process a magnetic strip card with data copied from a chip card through a point of service that isn't chip-enabled.
- You process a stolen-chip card that asks for a PIN, even if you have a chip-enabled point of service, but you accept a signature instead of the PIN.
- You only use a magnetic strip technology, and a consumer tries to claim someone else swiped a chip card in initiating a chargeback.

In short, even if you do fall for a chargeback scheme, you are protected from liability, although many retailers have been slow in adopting the new payment system. As of early 2016, only 37 percent of U.S. retailers were ready to accept chip cards. But increasingly, you can expect consumers to have these cards and more and more merchants to be able to process them. They are not perfect, but they do cut down on fraud—and since using them correctly transfers liability back to the credit card companies and banks, get up to date with this technology as soon as you can for retail or face-to-face transactions.

AVOIDING THE OVERPAYMENT CHARGE CARD SCAM

Another scam for merchants is the overpayment scam, whereby a customer or client asks to charge a card for more than is due and get the balance back in cash. While this is sometimes legitimate, such as when someone runs out of cash while traveling or goes to a local merchant to get some extra money, this can be a scam. An indication this is legit is when a person wants only a small amount back, even for a small charge.

The scam is related to one where the fraudster sends a victim a check, supposedly in payment for a certain amount, but asks the victim to wire the difference to someone else for some reason, such as to pay for travel expenses. Then the check turns out to be phony. In the case of a credit card overpayment, the victim pays out the difference and in addition is on the hook for the products or service because the fraudster has used a lost or stolen credit card.

An example of how this works is what happened to a barber in Florida. He received an e-mail asking if he could schedule and charge the haircuts for eight members of a groom's wedding party, who would be arriving at the shop by a private car. In this case, the barber became suspicious when he received an e-mail asking what credit card reader he used in processing his card sales. So he didn't respond, and the haircuts never happened. But the fraud prevention department of his credit card processor said this sounded like the classic overpayment scheme. Probably what would have happened is that after the barber did the haircuts, he would be asked to provide an additional cash payment for the driver. Thinking that he would be credited with the funds the next day, the barber would probably go along with the fraudster's request. But within two or three weeks, once his credit card processor learned the card was stolen, the barber would not only be out what he charged for the haircuts, but the extra money he charged on the stolen card, unless he used a chip-enabled reader for a chip-enabled card.

PAYING ATTENTION TO WARNING SIGNS AND RED FLAGS

Just as you might notice signs of problems ahead when a person pays you with a check, pay attention to similar warning signs and red flags when someone gives you a credit card that may open the door to a chargeback. In a retail setting, this might be a customer who wanders around and isn't sure what he or she wants. Another might be a customer who seems out of place with your usual customers, such as a customer who is dressed much more elegantly or is wearing shabby clothes. In that case, just pay more attention when the person pays with a credit card, and check if the card is signed. Whether it is or not, ask to see an ID, to see if the person matches photo. Also, if you are shipping products, be cautious if the person wants a much faster than usual delivery, and check that the address on the person's ID matches the address for the shipment—or ask to see other cards or documents with that address on it. There might be nothing wrong; a person may have just moved to another area or may have a different mailing address than a residence address, but the difference could also be a sign that this is a lost or stolen card, or the person may later claim he or she didn't receive the package, resulting in a chargeback. So be sure you make shipments with tracking, whether via the post office, UPS, or other delivery service. Also, be sure to get the person to sign to acknowledge the shipping arrangements. For instance, UPS has such a form that all customers sign.

Also pay attention to red flags, such as when someone asks you to perform certain services but asks to defer payment for a week or two, because the client is awaiting payments to himself. Sometimes this deferred payment works perfectly fine and your client appreciates your consideration in delaying payment so he can complete work that will result in his own future sales. But just be careful, and be sure to have a contract for the full job, or ask the client to sign an agreement about owing for the work. You have to play these kinds of situations by ear, based on whether you feel you can trust the client.

Another problem situation is where a person isn't sure what he or she wants or gives you unclear instructions on what to do. In some cases, the person may only be looking to you for advice and values your input and guidance, but in other cases, the person might remain confused and uncertain. Again, get any proposed work in writing so it is clear what you will be doing and for how much. Include something in your agreement about what happens if the person decides not to continue the work. Even if the person is paying you a retainer or you can charge for the work on a pay-as-you-go basis, it helps to have an understanding that you will get paid for work already done. Sometimes service providers also include a kill fee to compensate for any time they have set aside to work on the project, since they may have turned down other jobs in the process.

FIGHTING A CHARGEBACK

It used to be easier to win chargeback claims if you could show you did the work and you had some evidence that you did the work and delivered it to the customer or client, and he or she agreed for you to do it. At one time, a trail of e-mails and examples of the work you did or product you custom-created for the client would be enough.

But not so anymore if the customer or client claims fraud—not just disputes a charge—since the benefit of the doubt goes to the customer or client. That's why you need to have a clear agreement signed by the customer or client and provide proof of delivery. In some cases, clients falsely claiming fraud may lie, but if you can include evidence on the contract itself, such as the person's name, card number, V-code, and address linked to that card, that will help to support your evidence that the client did in fact agree to the terms.

In any case, you will be notified of the chargeback, usually by mail, and then you have about twenty-one days to respond. Be careful to keep your credit account information up to date, in case you move, because if you don't get the chargeback notice and don't respond to dispute it, that's the end of the case. Your client, however false the claim, has won.

You have an opportunity to provide whatever evidence you can to show you did the work or delivered the product as agreed. Aside from the original signed contract, include any e-mails between you and the client about the product or service to bolster your case. Send it to your credit card company or bank, preferably using tracking to be sure they get the material. Alternatively, you may be able to fax in the material.

Include page numbers, as well as a table of contents if you have extensive material to prove your case.

Next, your credit card provider or bank will review your materials, and if they think you have a convincing case, they will reverse the chargeback. However, the customer or client's credit card company or bank has a chance to respond. Or if you both have the same company or bank, you will each have a representative to battle your case. In either case, the client's credit card company or bank will dispute the chargeback reversal, and if the client continues to lie and claim to not have authorized the transaction or participated in it, normally the client's claim will be given extra weight. You may be able to swing the credit card rep or banker in your favor if you have a clearly signed agreement—perhaps even notarized—to further bolster your claim. Otherwise, even with an extensive e-mail trail showing your work on the project and your communications, the client might still falsely claim the work wasn't authorized or he or she didn't participate in the transaction. In short, though it isn't fair, unscrupulous clients can get away with cheating, as occurred in Gini's case, which opened this chapter. So your best protection is to avoid clients who might prove to be a problem in the future. Or perhaps consider these bad apples like merchants regard shrinkage. They focus on increasing their sales generally, knowing a small percentage of the sales won't be profitable, and they learn to live with that.

14

BALANCING THE NEED FOR SECURITY WITH BARRIERS TO SALES

Given all this concern with avoiding fraud from lost and stolen cards and false chargebacks, you need to find a happy medium to reduce your chances for fraud while not declining legitimate purchases, including making certain exceptions when someone you trust can't pay right now. Hiring some credit card protection services can help you in sharing the risk.

AVOIDING FALSE DECLINES

The problem of false declines is actually a serious one, since one of six cardholders had their cards declined because it was suspected of being fraudulent when it wasn't.[1] This has had a negative effect on future sales, since 39 percent of customers have abandoned their card, 25 percent have decreased their card usage, and 32 percent have given up shopping at a particular retailer for good. In fact, false declines account for more money lost—$118 billion—than actually lost to fraud—only about $9 billion. This problem has led MasterCard, among others, to seek to reduce these false declines.[2]

The reasons for these false declines run the gamut, but basically come down to a profile of a risky transaction. For example, a person has been traveling outside of their usual area or has spent more on a purchase than a pattern of purchases in the past. Another trigger might be when a person buys a series of products in one store within a short period of time. Whatever the reason, there is a card decline, which the person doesn't expect, knowing the card is good. In some cases, the problem can be remedied by using another card. But if the person doesn't have one or doesn't want to use it, the next step is to call the credit card company or bank and explain that the purchases are legitimate, and typically one has to provide evidence of making a series of purchases in the past. The process takes about fifteen minutes, including waiting for a customer service rep, and many customers don't want to bother and so abandon the sale.

However, MasterCard has been reducing the number of false declines with two products that combine technology and insights to reduce the number of clients who get falsely refused when they charge a card. One is Authorization IQ, which provides the merchant with insights about the cardholder to help the authorization center distinguish between authentic and fraudulent transactions. The other product is Assurance IQ, which helps merchants themselves make smarter decisions by providing them with a blended risk score for a transaction, which reduces the risk of thinking something could be a fraud when it isn't, such as when an affluent cardholder tends to "spend big and spontaneously, especially when traveling."

Another company that has been dealing with the problem of false declines is Signifyd, which has set up E-Commerce Assurance, a financial guarantee that protects online retailers in the case of chargebacks. It has the support of a full-service cloud platform that automates fraud prevention so businesses can increase sales and open new markets while they reduce their risk. As Steven Loeb writes: "Signifyd takes less than one second for a decision to be made on whether a charge is fraudulent or not, and it has seen approval rates greater than 90%."[3] By contrast, this approval rate has only been 86–88 percent, with someone manually reviewing the charge. The advantage for merchants in using this system is that Signifyd eliminates their usual chargeback rate of 0.5–1 percent, and the company also gets rid of the 0.7–1 percent that they spend in people costs to review transactions. Moreover, they eliminate the problem that many merchants face in declining 2–5 percent of the charges that are not fraudulent. The result is that merchants typically see their gross profits go up by 20 percent when they use the Signifyd system. Meanwhile the company itself has become increasingly successful. In

2015, it processed $5.6 billion in transactions from more than two thousand customers, and many companies on the Fortune 2000 and Internet Retailer Top 500 list now use them.

USING SMARTPHONE APPS

Another approach that reduces the risk of lost or stolen cards being used or cards being manufactured with stolen identities is using a smartphone, such as with a Chase Visa payment system. So instead of using a plastic credit card or debit card for retail purchases, consumers can now use smartphone apps that supposedly offer better security against theft. And an advantage for merchants is that they pay lower fees for these transactions than traditional credit card purchases. Moreover, pay apps have "zero merchant fraud liability," so if you do get a fraudulent purchase, the bank will pick up the charges.

The reason for the lower fraud potential is that these apps are on the customer's own smartphone, so even if a fraudster acquires a phone, which are normally very quickly reported, and can get past the PIN or password, they are unlikely to be able to use it for long to make any fraudulent purchases.

ASK TO SEE AN ID AND GET A SIGNED CARD

Although merchants aren't required to ask for any identification in processing a valid credit card and most major card networks have a no-signature required program for small purchases under a certain amount, such as $25 or $50, it can be an added protection against fraud. Often consumers will not put a signature on their cards and write "see ID," on the assumption that if a card is stolen, a merchant won't put through a transaction when the thief can't produce a valid ID. But this strategy doesn't normally work, because merchants "don't always look at the back of cards," according to Tamara E. Holms in an article for CreditCardsCom.[4] Also, many point-of-service terminals in stores allow customers to swipe their cards themselves and some contactless payment cards and smartphone payment systems enable customers to wave their card or phone one to two inches from a card reader to make a purchase. Moreover, when a card isn't signed, the thief can easily sign it if the card is lost or stolen, so there will be a match between the thief's signature and the signature on the card. An unsigned card is not considered valid by MasterCard or Visa, so if a customer or client hands you a card, see that it is signed, and if not, ask the customer or client to sign it. This will at least reduce your risk of getting lost or stolen cards, although if it's a chip card and you use a chip-enabled reader, the card issuer will pick up the fraudulent charges.

RECOGNIZE THE EVOLVING FACE OF FRAUD

At one time, much credit card fraud was due to lost or stolen cards, such as when a thief found a card or pulled a new card out of someone's mailbox and then called to activate the card, opening the door to using it for multiple purchases, until the real card owner discovered the theft. But now the problem is often a data breach, such as at a Target or Home Depot store, allowing thieves to create new cards using the customers' personal information. Or they make transactions where a card isn't present, such as online. The problem is how do you know? Especially with online transactions where you assume the risk if the transaction is later deemed fraud.

With card-present transactions, the best approach is to ask to see an ID and also to check the signatures on the card or on some other document, unless you already know the individual and have an ongoing relationship. If the card isn't present, a good approach is to have a conversation with the customer or client about the transaction, which can help you clarify what the person wants and sense if this is a legitimate purchase. If you sense that anything is wrong, you can also give the person a quick refund, and then don't' do the work or ship the products.

USING A VERIFIED CREDIT CARD ORDER FORM AND A VERIFICATION SERVICE

Another way to protect against fraud is to create a merchant account and set up a verified credit card order form on your website. Then, if a customer fills out this form and pays with a credit card, he or she can't later claim the payment is due to fraud.

Another approach is to use credit card verification, whereby you verify the credit card number at the point of purchase. Currently, Experian claims to be the only provider offering this. Essentially its special technology verifies the full credit number against a consumer's identity within seconds using its database of over 220 million consumers with credit cards. You will also get a fraud alert on closed accounts, lost or stolen credits cards, and statements from victims. The way the system works is a consumer visits your website and enters billing information and a credit card number on the checkout page of your merchant site. Presumably you could take someone's credit card information from a personal transaction and enter it yourself. Then, this information goes to Experian, which checks the information against its database to ensure that this is valid. Once the credit card number is verified, you receive a match code, and once this match is confirmed, you can process the order knowing that the credit card number does, in fact, belong to this consumer.

Besides a full match, you can get other match codes, including a P for partial match, a C for a match but the account is closed; L, a match, but the card is lost or stolen; E, an invalid card number, an X—no record or a security alert, and N—no match. You will also get information on the subscriber's name, the date they opened the card, the credit limit, and current balance. You can also get additional fraud alerts, such as a recent change of address, high-risk addresses, victim statements, and other potential indicators of identity theft activity. In this way, you can ensure that a person using a credit card actually owns that card.[5]

In short, do what you can to reduce your risk of fraud. You may not be able to reduce your risk entirely, but if you do what you can, including using a chip-card processor to handle in-person transactions, your bank or credit card company will pick up your losses. Plus some processors will offer you fraud insurance. For example, Signifyd (https://www.signifyd.com) offers online retailers a 100 percent guarantee against fraud. It has two plans. One is a 4 percent fee based on your orders, where the company will review your orders for free and then you pay for the company's help when you need it. The other is a 1 percent fee and leaving all of the fraud management to the company. You simply plug in the system to the most popular processing platforms. The company recommends whether to accept a credit card or not, and if the payment leads to fraud or a false chargeback, you are protected from losing any money.

OBTAINING, RETAINING, AND PROTECTING CREDIT CARD INFORMATION

While it is important to obtain complete credit card information to show authorization and help to defeat a fraudulent claim, it is also important to protect this information. You have to retain this information very carefully to protect it from being accessed by hackers and various types of software, such as malware that may try to obtain it and use it for credit card fraud and identity theft. One of the first major retailers to fall victim to this scam was Target stores in 2013, but since then, there have been reports in the news of other breaches, including Home Depot.

The breach can occur from hackers simply finding a trap door into the system. Also, cybercrooks have developed malware to steal credit card and debit card numbers from retailers. Essentially, malware is a type of software code that is planted into the system. Some of it can obtain information from the point of sale, such as ModPOS, and is so sophisticated that it is largely undetected by current antivirus scans. As described by one senior threat analyst at the cybersecurity firm iSight Partners, the cybersecurity industry considered ModPOS software "the most sophisticated point-of-sale malware we've seen to date. . . . Instead of being just one piece of software, it's actually a complex framework consisting of multiple modules and plugins. Those different pieces combine to collect a lot of detailed information about a target company, including everything from payment information directly about sales systems to the personal login credentials of executives."[6] One thing that has made it so difficult to get rid of this malware is that it uses various techniques, such as encryption, which scrambles up data, to hide itself, and uses file compression to evade investigators.

Commonly, the companies targeted are the biggest national companies, with millions of customers, although potentially any retailer or other company could be subjected to such an attack. However, companies have been taking steps to reduce their exposure to such malware and hackers, and you might use some of these techniques with the help of a cybersecurity expert who can guide you in what to do. For example, many companies have been using a more advanced form of encryption, such as point-to-point encryption, to protect consumer data. Point-to-point encryption protects payment card data as soon as a consumer uses a card in a point-of-sale machine, and this payment information is only unlocked when it is obtained by the payment processor. In fact, it is likely that almost all big retailers will have this equipment in place in 2016, since 41 percent of the members of the National Retail Federation had already installed such a system by September 2015, and 85 percent were projected to have installed such a system by the end of the year.

Such protections are critical, since even the new chip-enabled cards using a new chip-enabled processor could still be compromised by an infected point-of-sale processor used to process an online purchase. Plus, you have to remain alert to the potential for new cyber threats, since these are constantly evolving.

Though cyber criminals commonly use the data they gain from these cyber breaches to make credit card purchases or create brand new cards in the names of the customers whose data is stolen, they can also use this data to prospect for new customers who fall for their scheme. That's what happened to Walmart shoppers who were targeted with a fake mystery shopper program. Such scams typically invite victims to sign up to be a mystery shopper, and then they get paid with a phony check, from which they are supposed to wire an overpayment to a confederate who collects their money. But in the Walmart scam, customers are advised they have been randomly selected for Walmart's "quality control" mystery shopper program and that Walmart is sending them a check for $2,000. To activate it, they need to register on a website that asks for their personal information, including their name, address, phone number, and Social Security number. Moreover, the letter instructs them to deposit the check in their bank account, spend the money on anything at Walmart, and rate their experience in a survey. Of course, the victims think they are being shown a special appreciation by the company, but instead, once they deposit the check, the fraudsters drain their account. Figure 14.1 is a copy of the letter, which looks very official.

WALMART INC.

702 87H OF BENTONVILLE ARKANSAS 72716
coordinator@wmnewtalents.com
TEL: (501) 222-7753
FAX: (501) 222-8193

www.wmnewtalents.com

Use below assigned User ID and PASSWORD to sign into website.
This process is mandatory for all new participants.

USER ID #: 39967
PASSWORD: 1619536

Dear   <u>RE: ACCEPTANCE LETTER</u>
                                        Please activate the enclosed Payroll check online before depositing.

This is to inform you that based on the previous survey by our affiliate Consumer Survey and Quality Control Specialists, you indicated your interests in an additional income on a part time bases, you are hereby selected to participate in a paid **Quality Control Program**, as one of the Research Personnel selected under this program, you will be working as a **Consumer Service Evaluator** of some selected merchant outlets and service providers. This research program is a fully paid program and would become a permanent part time position for a selected few who are able to distinguish themselves in the course of this program. You will be assigned different jobs every week, for each job assignment, you will get paid different salary depending on the nature of the job assigned. Upon accepting this offer, you must keep your identity and assignment as a CONFIDENTIAL in order not to introduce any form of bias to the data you collect. There is no obligation as to how long you keep this job, you are allowed to quit whenever you want.

You will be required to complete a paid training assignment. This is a hands on self training designed to equip you with the knowledge necessary for you to effectively carry out your assignment(s) as an experienced research Personnel under this program.

Stores and organizations such as The Gap, Wal-Mart, Pizza Hut and amongst many others pay to shop in their establishments and report their experiences. On top of being paid for shopping you are also allowed to keep purchases for free.
Helping to drive exceptional bottom-line performance, nearly 800,000 shoppers have registered at our website, performing millions of BUY AND KEEP throughout Europe and North America. With our continual investment in the latest online and communication technologies, working as **Consumer Service Evaluator** is satisfying and rewarding experience.

<u>Breakdown of the enclosed check bearing the required funds to cover your first week</u>

1.   Participation Pay for first week...$350.00
2.   Stipulated Amount for Evaluation ....(See survey assignment # 1)
3.   Required Funds for retail shopping assignment ....(See survey assignment # 2)

Check activation: www.wmnewtalents.com
This process is mandatory to those that accept this offer and wish to participate in the ongoing **QUALITY CONTROL TRIAL ASSIGNMENT**
Get started, introduce your User ID# and password in the field indicated in our website, read carefully, follow instructions to activate your check online, after activation, deposit check into your regular bank account, when funds cleared and available, deduct your stipulated participation salary indicated, withdraw balance and get started immediately with assigned task.

If you are working with us for the first time, you MUST activate your check online for security and identification purposes, however, you may contact our webmaster or technical support if unable to activate online due to issues related to our website. **coordinator@wmnewtalents.com**

SURVEY ASSIGNMENT # 1: You will generate your assignment breakdown from our website **www.wmnewtalents.com**
Generate assignment only when money provided to cover expenses is ready in hand. Assignment generated must be completed within 24 hours. You will be disqualified automatically if assignment generated is not completed within stipulated time.

SURVEY ASSIGNMENT # 2: Generate your assignment in **www.wmnewtalents.com**
The items you buy are yours as a bonus and the funds needed to complete assignment will be determined when you generate assignment #2

EVALUATION/REPORTS: Evaluation/report form is available online, visit **www.wmnewtalents.com**
(User ID and password is required to Login) This online form must be completed after doing assigned evaluations/survey

Please note that it is mandatory that you report each completed job assignment to your coordinator immediately. Fax or scan all receipts, attach and send via e-mail for verifications purposes to: **scans@wmnewtalents.com**
Fax number will be provided after activation. Visit **www.wmnewtalents.com** and report your experience.
Job done but not reported will be considered **"NOT DONE"** and you will be disqualified automatically.

Sincerely,

Sandra P. Johnson
Director of Operations

IMPORTANT NOTICE

- *Personal information is NOT REQUIRED to do this job and you are not going be ask for such information.*
- *If your names are written wrongly in your payroll check, endorse reverse side with your correct names and sign behind it before depositing into bank account.*
- *Please note that it is mandatory that you e-mail coordinator to report each completed assignment. Job done but not reported for review will be considered "JOB NOT COMPLETED" And you will not be sent another job until further notice.*

Fax or scan all evaluation receipts immediately to e-mail: coordinator@wmnewtalents.com
Evaluation report is time sensitive; receipts must be submitted immediately after doing assigned evaluation to avoid disqualification.
Visit www.wmnewtalents.com and report your experience.
Read instructions carefully to complete assigned evaluation as instructed by coordinator.

Figure 14.1.   Please note this is not a letter from Walmart but a part of the scam mentioned in this chapter.

Obviously, consumers need to be alert to this variation of the mystery shopper scam. But merchants and service providers need to be aware of the potential of fraudsters to target you for the personal information about customers in your database. Thus, besides encrypting your data as best you can, you might send out announcements to your past customers to beware the different types of scams that have more recently been circulating.

COMMUNICATING WITH YOUR CUSTOMER

Communicating with your customers when you hear about scams that might affect them is one way to show your customers you care. You might also communicate with them about other topics, including everything from new products or services and industry trends to tips on protecting their credit. You can send this out as an occasional e-mail to customers on your mailing list or create a regular newsletter that might include articles on your blog plus other topics of interest, depending on your business. Such communications help to create a good ongoing relationship with your customers that can contribute to them wanting to buy from or work with you in the future.

In addition, you can discourage fraud by staying in contact with individual customers or clients who have made recent purchases and payments. Besides an initial e-mail advising your client that you will be charging a certain amount, send a follow-up e-mail to indicate that you have charged this amount for the service or product. You might even combine this with an evaluation form for the customer or client to share an opinion on your product or service, and if it's favorable, ask if you can use it as a testimonial. Should they be very busy or don't like to write anything, offer to write the letter for them, and then have them review and approve it or suggest any changes. You might even offer them a coupon for a discount on further products or services, or give them something for free.

Also in this communication, invite the customer or client to share any problems or advice on improving your product or service so you can seek to make changes accordingly. Even if the customer is satisfied, your offer can contribute to further customer satisfaction by showing your care and concern. When customers can contact you with any problems, you make it easier to work things out and thus avert potential claims of fraud from angry customers who feel they aren't being heard.

KEEP YOUR MERCHANT ACCOUNT OR ACCOUNTS CURRENT

If you move or make any major changes in your business, your merchant account provider or bank needs to know this so they can contact you about any fraud claim in a timely manner, giving you time to properly dispute the claim. Obviously, if you make any changes in your bank account information, your card issuer must be immediately informed of it, as they will be making deposits of credit payments to you into your account and deducting your own credit processing charges. Regular account maintenance checks every few months will also ensure that all of your payments and charges on your merchant account are in order and going to the right place.

AVOIDING PROBLEMS WITH MERCHANT ACCOUNTS AND CREDIT CARD PROCESSORS

Merchant accounts and credit card processing equipment are offered through various banks or independent companies with ties to banks, and their fees can vary widely. These fees can be complicated to calculate. They can vary based on the size of a charge, whether it is made on a U.S. or foreign card, and whether you include all the information about the cardholder requested, such as the V-code on the card and the cardholder's address and zip code, which can reduce the risk that it is a lost or stolen card. Additionally, there are standard interchange fees charged by other banks involved in the transaction, as well as fees for equipment rental and insurance, unless you purchase the equipment yourself. All of these fees and percentages can combine so you can end up with three different fees that together make up your monthly fee deducted from your bank—the interest on the charge you put through from your bank, the interest on your charge for the interchange rate, and the monthly charge for leasing your credit card equipment and any insurance added to that amount.

When you make your arrangements with your bank or a credit card processor, check into what these total fees are. Also, be aware of the potential for fraud—or at least for you to be exploited—in entering into these agreements. If you have a long-term relationship with your bank, you might not be aware that you are not only signing an agreement with your bank but also with the data processing service they use to handle processing your credit card income, and sometimes there can be problems with this service that the bank isn't even aware of. For example, the credit card account rep for one bank that used First Data for its processing was not aware of the hundreds of complaints against this company for misleading practices or its binding control for four years, even though the customer's agreement with the bank for the merchant account was only for three years. Plus this contract provided that "your lease payments will be due despite dissatisfaction with the Equipment for any reason." Moreover, should the merchant end the agreement with this merchant processing company, the obligation for the lease would still continue. First Data ultimately turned the contract into a debt on the merchant's credit card report. But the bank that made the arrangements with First Data was unaware of these contract provisions, which essentially created an adhesion contract that presumably couldn't be breeched. No wonder there were negative reviews from merchants and service providers on the RipOff Report and other consumer complaint sites. Here's a sampling of some of these complaints:

> Please beware if you do business with #First Data. . . . I am a small business owner and started a couple of years ago. For payment solution I contacted First Data. Their sales rep was all about helping small businesses grow. I clearly explained to the rep that I am trying a new business, so I don't want any contracts or lease. The rep explained that they help small businesses all the time, and even if we decide to close the store, there won't be any penalties. After two years of running the store, we decided to close down, as market had changed and there was less demand for the service we were offering. We returned the credit card machine.
>
> The credit machine was a small one, and not worth more than $75. When I called First Data, they said I have to pay them $660 and another $100 to close the account. After doing business with them for almost two years and paying them high credit card fees and charges, the company wants me to pay them $750 to close the ac-

count. They aren't willing to listen to anything. Their one liner is: "If you don't pay us $750, we will report it to the credit agency." When I told them about the promise their sales agent made, they replied that the agent may have lied to us. So you guys, First Data lie to get the business and then hold the personal credit hostage to extract more money."Ajay B. Carmichael, California, December 25, 2015 (RipOffReport).

First Data Corporation. They were supposed to give us information on savings for a merchant account, but then we realized they have made us sign a binding contract for 3 years and started charging us for equipment lease and merchant processing fee without our consent.

When the sales person came in our office and I met with him, I thought he was collecting information to provide us with a possible saving on our Credit Card merchant processing fees. However, only when we received a credit card processing machine in our office, we realized that he had actually made me sign a 3-year contract for leasing a machine which we do not even use in the first place. When we contacted them to let them know that this is a mistake and have them cancel it, they said it is a 3-year contract and there will be an early termination fee. This is while there were automatic monthly withdrawals from our account for about a year, and then once they could not withdraw anymore payment due to change in our bank account, they started their collection calls. We never used their equipment or their processing services, but they insisted on collecting from us the contract amount, this is while they had deceived us from day 1. Alec, Glendale, California, September 24, 2015 (RipOff Report).

First Data Global Leasing had no direct contract with me for providing equipment. The agreement was between them and the company with whom I contracted, Prestige. When Prestige broke its contract with me prior to my ever using its service once, I advised Global Leasing. However, GL continue to embezzle funds from my checking account when it had first-hand knowledge that it wasn't providing me with any service since my equipment had never been set up and it had already been advised by Prestige that the contract was dissolved. . . .

GL has no signed contract with me, never serviced me even once, knew I never used its equipment, knew the contractor no longer had a contract with me, so knew its service was unnecessary and still it charged me and considerably more than my present provider—at least 6 times more than what its equipment is worth on a monthly basis.

At some point GL turned my name in to the credit card companies in an effort to harm my credit rating and advised them that I owed it $3,000 which is totally fraudulent. This company needs to be investigated for unethical and illegal activity to harm businesses by forcing them to pay for service it knows it never provides. Holly Lane Gardens, Bainbridge Island, Washington, December 11, 2014.

There are hundreds of other complaints like this. From these complaints, it would seem that the First Data contract is unreasonable on its face, since it commits individuals to a contract to pay about $1,500 for equipment valued at $175, so even if the individual closes the business, becomes ill and can't conduct the business for a while, has no sales, or otherwise no longer needs the services or realizes it was a mistake to sign up for a merchant account, he or she is stuck with outrageously high costs that can't be stopped without being subjected to attempts at collection and possible litigation. This fee for leasing the equipment is in addition to the other monthly charges from the bank or other merchant account processing service, which charges its own interest fees and then adds the interchange fees.

Thus, when you arrange for a credit card merchant account, be sure to check with the bank or merchant account processing service providing the leased equipment and what the total of all your fees will be so you fully understand what you are paying and don't get caught up in an extended contract you can't get out of. Also, do some comparing apart from checking on what leasing service is involved, since interest rates and other fees also vary. And be aware of some recent processing alternatives, such as Square, that have an even lower interest rate than the traditional credit card processing services.

AVOIDING ONLINE AND OFFLINE CREDIT CARD FRAUD

Now that more business than ever is conducted online, it's especially important to be aware of criminals who charge as much merchandise as they can before the credit card is reported missing, or who later claim a chargeback on the grounds that they never received the merchandise. This kind of fraud largely involves merchants who have products, but it can also affect service providers whose services a client can later claim were not performed, since the burden is on companies to prove the customer claiming fraud actually received the merchandise or service. Following are a series of tips on what to do or not do so you can avoid the true criminals, not customers and clients who have legitimate disputes or who make errors using their cards. However, keep in mind that as you have more restrictions to stop or reduce fraud, you risk also discouraging sales, so you want to find a good balance between protecting yourself and not losing sales.

Avoiding Fraud through Chargebacks as Well as Other Types of Credit Card Fraud

Always ask to see IDs until you get to know the identities of individual customers. Check if there is a match between the photo on the card and the person presenting the card. If not, you can't take it, even if the person claims an innocent excuse, such as if he or she is a family member using the card. Use your judgment if the explanation seems valid, even ask for more identifying information to be sure; but if in doubt, don't accept the card. Ask to see the card and look for possible red flags, such as a worn-away signature line or a mismatch between the name on the card and the person's identification. It's also a warning sign if a customer resists handing you the card.

When taking a credit card over the phone or via e-mail, use an address verification service (AVS), which most credit card companies provide. Ask the cardholder for a billing address, zip code, and phone number, because that's the information the AVS system uses to check if there's a mismatch between the information the customer offers and the information on file with your credit processing company. A mismatch could be a warning, but there are many reasons why there could be a mismatch, such as the person has moved recently, is listed under a different variation of his or her name, or the information was entered with an error in spelling. Therefore, ask the customer to explain the difference and use your judgment on whether to accept the explanation or not.

Make sure you get the security code or verification number, which is on the back of the card, except for American Express, where it is on the front. (It's called a CVV2 by Visa, a CVC2 by MasterCard, and a CID by American Express.) Enter that when you process your card with your merchant account. This is added protection, because often criminals will take pictures of the front of the card, steal mail with credit card numbers, or steal a list of numbers with a skimming device. Since this code is not stored in the magnetic strip or embossed on the card thieves cannot easily get this number unless they actually have the card itself. So if a customer doesn't give you a CVV, or the card is declined because of a CVV mismatch, don't accept the sale.

Be cautious about any uncommonly large orders for a product. Often a criminal gets a list of stolen credit card numbers and has to use them as quickly as possible before the stolen numbers are reported. So the criminal will try to get as much merchandise as quickly as possible in order to sell it through a fence, flea market, or other means. Be even more wary if a customer wants expedited shipping for an uncommonly large order, since this might be an attempt to get the merchandise before the card is reported stolen.

If the billing and shipping address don't match, since criminals don't normally live or work in the same location as the cardholder, the shipping address might be the criminal's and the billing address that of the cardholder. Of course, sometimes a person could use a home address on their card and have another mailing address, and a customer might order something as a gift. So check to make sure it is a valid purchase before you ship anything. For example, call the customer's number to say you are just checking that you have the correct address for shipping and ask why the addresses are different. See if the customer's answer seems reasonable; probe some more if not sure; and, finally, don't ship if you have reservations, especially if this is an uncommonly large order.

Make sure there is a match between the customer's credit card billing address and IP (Internet Protocol) location, which indicates the address associated with their computer. They should be in the same general area. You can manually check an IP address at a site like IP-Lookup.net. Be especially careful if the IP address is from overseas, and the credit card address doesn't match. According to Anita Campbell,[7] you can cut down on the number of these iffy overseas transactions by restricting all IP addresses that originate from countries where you don't offer to ship products. You can program your site to keep such visits from checking out in the first place, and some e-commerce software platforms enable you to block IP addresses without requiring you to need custom programming.

Another way to detect a possible fraudulent transaction is to research the billing or shipping address on the order. According to Campbell, you can use Google maps or Zillow to determine if the address is legitimate. Another method is using ZabaSearch to check that the customer actually lives at the address you are questioning or use an address verification offered by many payment services and credit card processing companies.[8]

Check with your payment service or credit card processing company to see if they have an IP verification tool so you can check on the credit cardholder's IP. Usually the IP address will show up next to the customer's actual address. This can help you see if the card is being used by a purchaser who is overseas or from a suspicious source.[9]

Watch out for suspicious e-mail addresses that can suggest you are receiving a fraudulent credit card transaction. If you have an e-mail that's a jumble of letters and numbers, this could be a red flag, since names with no apparent connection to a customer's name or have random characters could be an attempt to mask the real customer's identity. Check with a phone call to the prospective client. Most people have free e-mail addresses, such as at Gmail, Hotmail, Yahoo!, and AOL, but these free e-mails make it easy to conceal the customer's identity. Thus, checking other information to be sure that person is who he or she claims is imperative when dealing with customers by e-mail.

Keep a record of any credit card numbers entered into your processing service, and look for duplicates or multiple entries by the same customers. As Campbell points out, scammers will attempt to make as many transactions as they can on one card or multiple cards. So if there are four or five or more attempts, that's a sign it could be a fraud—so don't send any merchandise without further checking. In fact, the bank that issued the card will often place a block on a card after multiple entries, as one woman found after she made several dozen purchases of ninety-nine cents each for photos for a project. She had to talk to the bank repeatedly, which repeatedly put up blocks and finally said she could only make up to thirty purchases on her card in a single day. So multiple purchases could be legitimate, but in many cases, they are a sign to watch out.[10] As recommended by Instamerchant, you can also create a negative database to identify high-risk transactions, and then block specific credit card numbers in your system so you don't process these orders.[11]

Look out for repeated attempts with the same credit card number, in which someone—or even a credit card generation software program such as CreditMaster—repeatedly enters the number with varying names and expiration dates until the transaction goes through. The names might be varied because a person might have different variations on their name, such as Fred Smith, Fred J. Smith, and Frederick Smith. But the name on the card must correctly match when the name on the card is entered with that number. Given the speed with which these software programs work, the number of unauthorized entries can be huge. For example, one small merchant reported to Instamerchant that he had only three or four sales in a period, but three thousand authorization attempts.[12]

Restrict the number of times a user can incorrectly enter a credit card number, and don't accept an order if a potential customer goes over that number of attempted transactions. The reason for doing this is that sometimes fraudster use a software script where they try a series of credit card numbers in succession, and you may get charged a fee for each declined transaction. If you restrict the number of attempts, you will avoid or reduce the extra charges for declines.

Consider using a fraud profiling service, such as MaxMind. According to Campbell,[13] these services "cross-reference IP addresses, names, previous purchases, and more." Another advantage of these services is that they study per-purchase behaviors, so they can provide a "more informed assessment around each transaction" and can thereby identify high-risk transactions. Some e-commerce platforms, such as Volusion, even offer add-on fraud profiling services that work with their software.[14]

When you ship orders, use tracking numbers provided by the post office, UPS, or Federal Express, and require a signature, especially for expensive items. While this might discourage some criminals, those with confederates and arrangements with shipping services might still be able to take deliveries before they conveniently go out of business, having gotten merchandise from multiple merchants for free. At least, you can still use this tracking information with regular customers who claim they never received the merchandise to show you did ship it.

If you are sending out merchandise or performing a service after processing the credit card, not on-site, obtain the cardholder's signed proof of delivery.

Use the correct wording on the transaction receipt, such as "delayed delivery," "deposit," or "balance," to show what you received and what the customer expects. While you can process "delayed delivery" transactions before you actually deliver the goods or service, you can't process a "deposit" or "balance" transaction receipt before you actually deliver the goods or services. You can protect yourself if you put through the payment before a "delayed delivery," to make sure the charged amount actually went through.

While installment transactions are less likely to be a source of fraud, you can avoid unwarranted chargebacks by advising your customer in writing the terms of the transaction, including shipping and handling charges and any applicable tax. Don't process the first payment on the installment agreement before you deliver the goods and service, unless you also have an agreement that this will be a "delayed delivery" to begin the installment agreement.

Prepayment agreements are also less likely to be fraudulent, though again, handle these correctly to avoid chargebacks. To process a prepayment transaction, advise your customer or client that you will be billing him or her immediately. You can also process a full payment for custom-ordered merchandise, and it is a good idea to do so to avoid not getting the balance if the customer changes his or her mind about the order. Just provide the customer with a receipt indicating that the order is paid in full with no returns, since it is custom ordered, and make sure the customer signs the agreement.

Make sure your whole website and e-commerce system is secure to avoid or reduce the chance of cyber attacks, which can hack into any information stored on your website. As Anita Campbell points out, cyber attacks against small businesses are increasing because these websites are viewed as being more vulnerable than the sites of larger corporations. To this end, make sure your systems and services are PCI-compliant, which means that they meet the standards of the credit card industry for e-commerce transactions. Both Visa and MasterCard have lists of certified PCI-compliant providers, and the major e-commerce software platforms or shopping cart providers have information on their websites about what you need to do to be PCI-compliant. In fact, you can see a business guide to data security that Visa offers, and Master-Card has online fraud-prevention training for merchants, too.[15]

Consider using a "trust mark" security service for your e-commerce website. This service will search each day for malware and vulnerabilities to help you avoid or quickly spot any problems so you can fit them. Some examples of these services include Truste, Verisign, or McAfee Secure.[16]

Regularly update whatever software you use, since these updates will often include security patches to help you avoid breaches to your site. As long as you have vulnerability in any of your software programs, even if not in your e-commerce software, it can open up a door for cybercriminals to access your customer data and steal credit card numbers and other information, which can result in even more damages than a fraudulent credit card transaction.[17]

Ask for your customer's telephone number during a transaction so you can call to verify the order and telephone number, especially in the case of a large order. If the person who answers at that number doesn't recognize the name of the customer, it is likely to be a fraudulent order.[18]

Do everything you can to validate an order before you ship it. For example, when the person placing the order is not there in person and it's a sizeable order, ask the customer to fax copies of both sides of the credit card, or instead of faxing, the customer might scan and e-mail you a PDF with this information. Another suggestion is to ask the customer to provide a copy of his or her state-issued identification card, such as a driver's license, which provides added proof that the customer really does have a credit card. If a fraudster does not know all of this information or have it in his or her possession, he or she may give up.[19]

If you are suspicious about a potential fraud, another suggestion is that you can call the card-issuing bank and ask them to make a courtesy call to the customer to verify the charge.[20] Or use an address verification service, which will compare the billing address provided by the customer to the address in the bank's database. According to Visa, using this verification approach can reduce chargebacks by up to 26 percent.[21]

More Tips for Avoiding Both Online and Point-of-Sale Credit Card Fraud

- Consider not accepting credit cards from customers, unless they provide you with full information, including their complete address and phone number.
- If you aren't able to deliver the merchandise or service immediately at the point of sale, require the cardholder to sign a proof of delivery upon receiving the merchandise or service. That way the customer can't later claim he or she didn't receive the merchandise or service.
- If a customer asks for a refund, quickly process the refund using the same card number as in the original sale. Do not give a customer a refund by cash or check, since if it's a fraudulent transaction with a stolen credit card number, you will not only not get the original payment, but you will be out whatever you paid in cash or by check.
- Clearly state your return policy for any customer, and if you have a restocking or return processing fee, state that, so at least you don't end up being charged for the original processing fees and any return fees by your credit card company. This can also avoid the situation where a customer buys something to use briefly and return without having to pay for it.
- Avoid in-house misuse of your merchant account by limiting the number of people who have access to your account to process credit cards, and make sure you can trust them by doing a full background and reference check before you hire them or arrange to share the credit card processing service with them. For example, if you are making the equipment available to someone who doesn't have a merchant account, say someone who wants to sell products or services at a local fair, check up on what the person is doing. Review the batch reports that come in each night to see that their claimed orders match the totals on your nightly batch report when there are sales. If there are mismatches, find out why, and if the person doesn't have a good explanation, then fire an employee or end the access of a partner or associate using the processing system.
- Make sure that all the information on your sales draft is complete, accurate, and legible. If needed, check the ink cartridge or ribbon on your printer and install a new cartridge or ribbon if the ink or ribbon is running out. If your roll of paper for your processing equipment

runs out, get it from your local office supply store or call your processing service and order from them (usually they come ten or twenty to a box).

- Only process one transaction at a time through your credit card processing terminal. If a customer makes more than one purchase or makes two purchases for the same dollar amount within the same day, create one invoice per transaction to describe each purchase.
- If a transaction is declined, do not continue to seek authorization for it or reduce the amount requested. Instead, let the customer know and ask for another credit card. In some cases, a customer will advise you that the money will be available the next day, so you can try again. In any event, don't deliver any product or service until the sale for the full amount is authorized.
- Look for areas where your business is vulnerable and create policies or procedures to deal with these weaknesses, either by you or your employees. For example, notice if your employees always check credit card signatures or check if the driver's license photo matches the person in front of them. Train your employees on these procedures and monitor them to make sure they are carrying out these policies.

More Tips for Avoiding Online Credit Card Fraud

- Be cautious about late-night orders or orders from certain countries. Fraud is greater at night and from some countries or regions, including Israel, Eastern Europe, and South America, according a list of tips on avoid fraud from Instamerchant.[22]
- You can accept checks online through a service like VirtualCheck, which can confirm that the check is valid and there is enough into the account to pay it. As an alternative, if you get an online check, you can call the cardholder's bank, verify the account number, account holder's name, and if there are sufficient funds to clear the check.
- Regularly change your online merchant account password, and regularly check that your totals reported online match your receipts and daily reports of sales. If not, figure out the reason for any discrepancy and correct that going forward.

More Tips for Avoiding Point-of-Sale Retail Frauds

- Check the cardholder's signature to see that it is the same as the name on the card. For example, you might ask the customer to sign a receipt for purchase or a request for information, and then you can look at the two signatures to see if they match. If not, you can explain the problem, see if the customer provides a reasonable explanation, or ask for another credit card or some type of identification to protect yourself. At this point, fraudsters using someone else's card will typically decide not to go through with the sale or even take off to avoid being caught by law enforcement.
- Try calling the customer by the name on the card. If the cardholder does not respond or at least look around to see why someone is calling his or her name, that's a warning sign, though there can be other reasons, such as a hard-of-hearing customer.
- If you take checks, you can make arrangements with a check-authorization service, where you can put the check through a check reader and the service can tell if the check is legitimate and if there is enough money to cover it and give you an authorization number. If there is any problem with the check, the service will reject it. In some cases, the check reader will actually debit the check from the person's bank, void the check, and return it to the customer. Many of the bigger stores now use this kind of processing.
- If you can't swipe a card through your terminal, Instamerchant recommends that you obtain a manual imprint of the card. Get your customer to sign it and note the authorization code and purchase amount on the slip. This way you can prove that the actual card was present at the point of sale, which is important if a dispute arises or if a customer fraudulently seeks to claim not being present during the sale. Imprinting the card also enables you to capture the imprinted data from the front of the card, although you can't input the data on the magnetic strip on the back of the card.[23]
- Check the security features on each credit card to see that they operate the way they normally do, which will help to show that the card is valid or not. For instance, a hologram should change color in the light, and there should be a nonerasable signature line. If anything appears wrong, such as a signature that seems to have been erased and a new one written over it, or a signature that has been

altered with a different pen stroke or slightly different color, don't accept the card.

- Check that the signature on the receipt matches the signature on the back of the card. If there is any discrepancy, ask the customer to explain. If the customer gives a reasonable explanation, ask the customer for further identification, such as a driver's license. Or if you don't trust the customer's explanation, don't accept the card.
- If you get a card that says "See ID" on the signature strip or isn't signed, be cautious. Sometimes a customer will not sign a card or ask a merchant or service provider to check their ID or ID photo because they think this is a way to protect themselves against forgeries. But both Visa and MasterCard have a policy that merchants should not accept unsigned cards, so you may be liable for the charge if the card is unsigned.[24] Also, checking IDs may not be legal in some states. However, as a practical matter, merchants commonly ask to see an ID, and legitimate customers have no problem showing it. On the other hand, sophisticated fraudsters could create their own phony IDs. Thus, not every fraud prevention technique is foolproof, but at least you should be able to reduce the potential for fraud.

PROTECTING YOUR BUSINESS AGAINST DATA THEFT

The same kind of steps that you take to protect your data against theft for credit card fraud can also be used to protect against data theft generally. In fact, business owners are required to protect customer and employee personal information and can face significant state and/or federal fines if they don't and this information leaks. As a result, they can face legal penalties and lawsuits not only if this stolen information is used to perpetrate fraud, but also if it is used for other purposes, including revealing private information about customers, clients, and others.

Under the circumstances, the National Federation of Independent Retailers recommends doing the following:[25]

- Encrypt any data in laptop computers, which are very vulnerable to theft, and encrypt the full-disk rather than just the file. Also password-protect the computer.
- Encrypt any data in desktop computers, too.

- Shred all sensitive documents and keep them in locked containers until they are shredded.
- If you don't do the shredding yourself, assign the task to specific employees and have them verify and record that they have done it. Establish appropriate checks and balances to make sure that the employees successfully carry out this mission, such as by "assigning employees to oversee those who have access to, or handle, sensitive information."[26]
- Stay current with the latest technologies, such as firewalls, antivirus programs, and spyware. Cybercriminals continue to develop workarounds, so they may still be able to get through. A particular risk is keylogger programs, which are designed to read keystrokes, and transmit that information back to the hackers. These programs, much like other malware, spyware, or ransomware, can infect your computer when you visit a dangerous website, open an attachment, follow a link, or even download an MP3. The keyloggers record your unencrypted keystrokes allowing fraudsters to learn passwords and file names, giving them an open door to anything they want from your computer.

REPORTING FRAUD WHEN YOU SEE IT

Call your credit card processing company if any credit card transactions seem suspicious. This can help the company find out if a card or card number has been stolen or used for fraudulent transactions, and it can red flag that card number if used again.

Also, report the fraud to the appropriate agencies and reporting services to help law enforcement and organizations fighting identity fraud. You might receive restitution for your losses as well. Fraud reports can also alert other business owners to potential fraud activity and possibly lead to the fraudster's arrest and conviction or loss of a professional or business license.

Some of the sites that can help you avoid scams—and where you can report suspected frauds are:

- The National Fraud Information Center (http://www.fraud.org).
- The Federal Trade Commission (http://www.ftc.org).

- The Better Business Bureau (http://www.bbb.org).

BE CAREFUL ABOUT WHO YOU EMPLOY

Finally, as much as you have to be careful about the potential for fraud coming from cybercriminals and local fraudsters, you have to be careful about your employees, too, who might facilitate the efforts of others outside the company, either knowingly or unknowingly. And some might be fraudsters themselves, using the information obtained through your company to commit fraud from within.

For example, the National Federation of Independent Businesses warns that "internal threats . . . can go on for a long time without being detected."[27] Another danger is temporary workers who gain access to your company when they fill in for a regular employee who is ill or on vacation. Once they are working for you, they can execute their scheme of stealing personal information.

If employees haven't been trained sufficiently or are left on their own, unaccountable to management, they may mishandle data. Their lack of knowledge can provide an accidental opening for a fraudster to sweep in and get data from your company for credit card fraud, identity theft, or other criminal uses for that data.

Thus, it's a good idea to work alongside your employees from time to time, even if you think they are trustworthy, because they are in an ideal position to steal information from you. They are already familiar with your procedures, have access to your computers with files on them, and often can readily take what they need out with them on a DVD or flash drive, or send it to a cloud storage area they control. Usually, they are in a good position to disguise what they have been doing. Often they don't get caught until they leave for another company.

NOTES

FOREWORD

1. https://www.fbi.gov/scams-safety/fraud/internet_fraud.

I. PROTECTING YOURSELF FROM CREDIT CARD FRAUD AS A CONSUMER

1. "Credit Cards: Skimming Off the Top," *Economist*, February 15, 2014, https://www.nilsonreport.com/upload/pdf/Skimming_off_the_top_-_The_ Economist.pdf.
2. "Credit Card Skimming Scams Overseas: Five Tips to Avoid Getting Caught Out," *Stuff*, http://www.stuff.co.nz/travel/news/77272469/credit-card-skimming-scams-overseas-five-tips-to-avoid-getting-caught-out.
3. "Credit Cards: Skimming Off the Top."
4. Ibid.

2. DON'T GET SKIMMED—AND USING THE NEW CHIP CARDS

1. Alexis McAdams, "Police Continue to Find Dozens of Credit Card Skimmers at Gas Pumps around Central Indiana," Fox59, February 20, 2016, http://fox59.com/2016/02/20/police-continue-to-find-dozens-of-credit-card-skimmers-at-gas-pumps-around-central-indiana.

2. "Credit Card Skimming Scams Overseas: Five Tips to Avoid Getting Caught Out," *Stuff*, February 25, 2016, http://www.stuff.co.nz/travel/news/ 77272469/credit-card-skimming-scams-overseas-five-tips-to-avoid-getting-caught-out.

3. Nick Clemente, "5 Ways to Protect Yourself Against Debit Card Fraud," *Forbes*, May 21, 2015.

4. Ashley Knight, "When to Use a Credit Card vs. Debit Card," WKRG, March 5, 2016, http://wkrg.com/2016/-3/05/when-to-use-a-credit-card-vs-debit-card.

5. Ibid.

6. Matt Fountain, "Police Pursue Thieves Who Use 'Skimming' Devices to Steal Credit and Debit Card Information," *San Luis Obispo.com*, March 5, 2016, http://www.sanluisobispo.com/news/local/crime/article64372312.html.

7. Ibid.

8. Ibid.

3. WAYS TO GUARD YOUR PERSONAL FINANCIAL INFORMATION

1. "How to Keep Your Personal Information Secure," Federal Trade Commission, Consumer Information, https://www.consumer.ftc.gov/0272-how-keep-your-personal-information-secure.

2. Encryption Software Review, http://encryption-software-review. toptenreviews.com/.

3. "How to Keep Your Personal Information Secure," Federal Trade Commission, Consumer Information, https://www.consumer.ftc.gov/articles/ 0272-how-keep-your-personal-information-secure.

4. Ibid.

4. CREDIT CARD OFFERS

1. Consumer Complaint Database, http://www.consumerfinance.gov/ complaintdatabase.

2. Chris Morton, "Capital One Is The Most Complained-About Credit Card Company," *Consumerist*, January 15, 2014, https://consumerist.com/ 2014/01/15/capital-one-is-the-most-complained-about-credit-card-company.

3. Consumer Financial Protection Bureau, http://www.consumerfinance. gov/complaint.

4. Chris Morton, "Capital One Is the Most Complained-About Credit Card Company," *Consumerist*, January 15, 2014, https://consumerist.com/2014/01/15/capital-one-is-the-most-complained-about-credit-card-company.

5. "Merrick Bank—Credit Card Fraud," http://merrick-bank.pissedconsumer.com/credit-card-fraud-20160307804699.html.

6. "Merrick Bank: Money Hungry Company," http://merrick-bank.pissedconsumer.com/money-hungry-company-20160304803076.html.

7. "Merrick Bank Not a Credible Bank," http://merrick-bank.pissedconsumer.com/merrick-bank-not-a-credible-bank-20151209748225.html.

8. "Merrick Bank—Crappy Bank and Shady Business Practices," http://merrick-bank.pissedconsumer.com/crappy-bank-and-shady-business-practices-20150223599468.html.

9. "Barclays Bank Delaware Barclaycard Bait & Switch Annual Fee Wilmington Nationwide," http://www.ripoffreport.com/r/Barclays-Bank-Delaware/nationwide/Barclays-Bank-Delaware-Barclaycard-Bait-amp-Switch-Annual-Fee-Wilmington-Nationwide-1145153.

10. "Barclaycard us Barclays Bank Damaged Credit History Without a Cause Nationwide," http://www.ripoffreport.com/r/barclaycard-us/nationwide/barclaycard-us-Barclays-Bank-Damaged-Credit-History-without-a-cause-Nationwide-1203867.

11. "Capital One—Shady Practices," http://capital-one.pissedconsumer.com/capital-one-shady-practices-they-don-t-close-your-credit-card-20160312808535.html.

5. AVOIDING FREE TRIAL AND SPECIAL DISCOUNT SCAMS

1. Federal Trade Commission, "'Free' Trial Offers?" https://www.consumer.ftc.gov/articles/0101-free-trial-offers.

2. Ibid.

3. Kathy Kristof, "Nation's Top Scam? Free Trial Offer," CBS News, January 7, 2010. http://www.cbsnews.com/news/nations-top-scam-free-trial-offer.

6. CREDIT CARD AND SERVICE SCAMS

1. Federal Trade Commission, "Credit Repair: How to Help Yourself," https://www.consumer.ftc.gov/articles/0058-credit-repair-how-help-yourself.

2. Federal Trade Commission, "Credit Repair Scams," https://www.consumer.ftc.gov/articles/0225-credit-repair-scams.

3. Federal Trade Commission et al. vs. All Us Marketing LLC et al., No. 6:2015cv01016, Document 132 (M.D. Fla. 2016), "Stipulated Order for Permanent Injunction and Final Settlement," http://law.justia.com/cases/federal/district-courts/florida/flmdce/6:2015cv01016/312225/132/.

7. PROTECTING YOUR CREDIT CARD

1. Federal Trade Commission, "Disputing Credit Card Charges," https://www.consumer.ftc.gov/articles/0219-disputing-credit-card-charges.

8. PHISHING AND OTHER ONLINE FRAUDS

1. Sean Butler, "Scammers Pose as Company Execs in Wire Transfer Spam Campaign," *Symantec Official Blog*, October 28, 2014, http://www.symantec.com/connect/blogs/scammers-pose-company-execs-wire-transfer-spam-campaign.

2. Brett M. Christensen, "IRS Warns about Phishing Scam," *Hoax Slayer*, March 8, 2016, http://www.hoax-slayer.net/irs-warns-about-ceo-phishing-scam-email.

3. Wikipedia, "Phishing," https://en.wikipedia.org/wiki/Phishing.

4. *Symantec Intelligence Report*, January 2015, https://www.symantec.com/content/en/us/enterprise/other_resources/b-intelligence-report-01-2015-en-us.pdf.

5. "What Is Phishing?," *Phishing.org*, http://www.phishing.org.

6. "The Cost of Phishing? More Than You Think," *Security Ledger*, August 26, 2015, https://securityledger.com/2015/08/the-cost-of-phishing-more-than-you-think.

7. "10 Ways to Avoid Phishing Scams," *Phishing.org*, http://www.phishing.org/scams/avoid-phishing.

8. Wikipedia, "Ransomware," https://en.wikipedia.org/wiki/Ransomware.

9. "Alert (TA16-091A) Ransomware and Recent Variants," US-CERT, https://www.us-cert.gov/ncas/alerts/TA16-091A.

10. Ibid.

11. Ibid.

12. Brad Jones, "Email Scam Petya Locks Down PCs until a Ransom Is Paid," *Digital Trends*, March 25, 2016, http://www.digitaltrends.com/computing/petya-malware/.

13. "Alert (TA16-091A) Ransomware and Recent Variants."

14. Marie Keyworth and Matthew Wall, "The 'Bogus Boss' Email Scam Costing Firms Millions," BBC, January 8, 2016, http://www.bbc.com/news/business-35250678.

9. WHAT TO DO IF YOU ARE A VICTIM OF CREDIT CARD FRAUD OR PERSONAL IDENTITY THEFT

1. Laura Shin, "'Someone Had Taken Over My Life': An Identity Theft Victim's Story," *Forbes*, November 18, 2014, http://www.forbes.com/sites/laurashin/2014/11/18/someone-had-taken-over-my-life-an-identity-theft-victims-story.

2. Nina Crisculo, "Child ID Theft: Up to 18 Years of Undetected Credit," WishTV, March 3, 2016, http://wishtv.com/2016/03/03/child-id-theft-up-to-18-years-of-undetected-credit/.

3. Shin, "'Someone Had Taken Over My Life.'"

4. Ibid.

5. Jonnelle Marte, "7 Ways to Avoid Identity Theft This Holiday Season," *Washington Post*, November 24, 2015.

6. "Identity Theft," Reddit, https://www.reddit.com/r/personalfinance/wiki/identity_theft.

7. "Identity Theft and Credit Card Fraud—How to Protect Yourself," *Wall Street Journal*, December 17, 2008. http://guides.wsj.com/personal-finance/credit/how-to-protect-yourself-from-identity-theft.

12. THE POTENTIAL FOR CREDIT CARD FRAUD

1. Rick Rojas and Al Baker, "New York Police Focus on Fraud Involving Credit Cards," *New York Times*, September 10, 2015, http://www.nytimes.com/2015/09/11/nyregion/new-york-police-focus-on-fraud-involving-credit-cards.html.

2. Rocco Parascandola et al., "Identity-Thieving Brooklyn Couple Arrested in $100G Credit Card Scam," *New York Daily News*, March 1, 2016.

3. John Harper, "New Yorkers Charged in Three-State Credit Card Theft Ring Targeting Cleveland-Area Giant Eagle Stores," *Cleveland.com*, March 2,

2016, http://www.cleveland.com/crime/index.ssf/2016/03/new_yorkers_
charged_in_three-s.html.

4. Julia Jacobo, "Miami Couple Charges with $2 Million Identity Theft
Fraud, Authorities Say," *Good Morning America*, April 7, 2016, http://abcnews.
go.com/US/miami-couple-charged-million-identity-theft-fraud-authorities/
story?id=38222486.

5. Andy Polhamus, "Have You Seen This Guy? Cops Say He Committed
Credit Card Fraud," *NJ.com*, http://www.nj.com/gloucester-county/index.ssf/
2016/03/have_you_seen_this_guy_cops_say_he_committed_credi.html.

13. AVOIDING CHARGEBACK FRAUDS

1. "How Companies Can Protect Themselves against Chargebacks,"
Chargify, April 12, 2010, https://www.chargify.com/blog/how-companies-can-
protect-themselves-against-chargebacks.

2. Chris A. Jenny and William R. West, "To Swipe or Not to Swipe—That
Is Retailer's Current Credit Card Dilemma," *National Law Review*, http://
www.natlawreview.com/print/article/to-swipe-or-not-to-swipe-retail-s-current-
credit-card-dilmma.

14. BALANCING THE NEED FOR SECURITY WITH BARRIERS TO SALES

1. Steven Loeb, "Signifyd Raises $20M to Stop False Credit Card De-
clines," *Vator*, February 26, 2016, http://vator.tv/news/2016-02-25-signifyd-
raises-20m-to-stop-false-credit-card-declines.

2. Pymnts, "MasterCard's Aim to Reduce False Declines," *Pyments.com*,
February 19, 2016, http://www.pymnts.com/news/merchant-innovation/2016/
mastercards-aim-to-reduce-false-declines/.

3. Loeb, "Signifyd Raises $20M."

4. Tamara E. Holmes, "Sign Your Credit Card, Don't Write 'See ID,' *Cred
Cards.com*. http://www.creditcards.com/credit-card-news/sign-or-write-see-
ID-1282php.

5. "Credit Card Verification," Experian, http://www.experian.com/
decision-analytics-credit-card-verification.html

6. Andrea Peterson, "Just in Time for Holiday Shopping: Researchers
Warn of Stealthy, Credit-Card-Stealing Malware," *Washington Post*, November 24, 2015.

7. Anita Campbell, "10 Tips for Preventing Online Credit Card Fraud," *Small Business Trends*, September 12, 2013, http://wmallbiztrends.com/2013/09/tips-prevent-online-credit-card-fraud.html.

8. Ibid.

9. Mark Welling, "Credit Card Processing: How Business Can Protect Themselves from Fraud," *Credit Card Processing Review*, May 29, 2014, http://credit-card-processing-review.toptenreviews.com/credit-card-processing-how-businesses-can-protect-themselves-from-fraud.html.

10. Campbell, "10 Tips for Preventing Online Credit Card Fraud."

11. Ibid.

12. Ibid.

13. Ibid.

14. Ibid.

15. Ibid.

16. Ibid.

17. Ibid.

18. Ibid.

19. Megan R. Stell, "Credit Card Fraud: 5 Steps to Protect Your Business," National Federation of Independent Business, March 6, 2012, http://www.nfib.com/content/resources/money/credit-card-fraud-5-steps-to-protect-yourbusiness-29075/.

20. Ibid.

21. Ibid.

22. "Stopping Fraud When Accepting Credit Cards Online," Instant Merchant, http://www.instamerchant.com/avoid-creditcard-fraud.html.

23. Campbell, "10 Tips for Preventing Online Credit Card Fraud."

24. Elaine Pofeldt, "Protecting Your Business from Credit Card Fraud," *Creditards.com*, http://www.creditcards.com/credit-card-news/protect-store-credit_card-fraud-1585.php.

25. National Federation of Independent Retailers, "Protecting Your Small Business Against Data Theft," http://www.nfib.com/article/?msid=45069.

26. Ibid.

27. Ibid.

INDEX

ACI Worldwide, 4

action item, 147; after automatic debit scams, 89; after card is lost, misplaced or stolen, 147–148; after free trial scam, or other, 150–151; after identity theft, 152–154; before identity theft, 151–152; after incorrect charge, 149–150

address verification service (AVS), 204; to do-it-yourself, 205–206

advance-fee loan scam, 97–98

advertising, as scam, 69–70

Aite Group, 4

Amazon: multifactor authentication on, 159; phisher impersonating as, 131–132

annualcreditreport.com, 76

annual percentage rate (APR), 92

The Anti-Phishing Working Group (APWG), 139

Apple Pay, 160

APWG. *See* The Anti-Phishing Working Group

Assurance IQ, 192

ATM: chip card at, 159; skimmer on, 5, 10, 12–13; suspicion at, 18–19

Authorization IQ, 192

automatic debit scam, 87–88; protection against, 88; "what to do" after, 89

AVS. *See* address verification service

Barclays Bank, 42–43; complaints against, 45–48

Beau Derma and Revita Eye Scam, 57–63, 58; product name change to, 67

Bernard, Rondon, 178–179

The Better Business Bureau, 40; on Barclays Bank, 45–48; on BeauDerma and Revita Eye Scam, 58, 62; imposter as, 98; website for, 42, 72, 73, 215

billing errors: cancel orders, refund for, 103–104; credit card dispute from, 101–102; debit card dispute from, 103; merchandise never received, dispute over, 100–101

Bitcoin, 140–141

Bitlocker, 152

bogus boss scam, 144–145

Caballero, Raymond, 178–179

Campbell, Anita, 205–208

cancellation: billing errors, refund for, 103–104; of preapproved credit offers, 51–53

Capital One, 17, 38, 42–43; complaints against, 48–50

card information: consumer protection of, 116–118; for merchant protection, 196–199; reduce, number of cards, 24; victimization, theft of, 5–6

card reader skimmer. *See* skimming

Card Security Code (CVV), 9, 205

Lightning Source UK Ltd.
Milton Keynes UK
UKOW04n2240151217
314508UK00014B/1252/P